The Ones On the 'Other' Side

PAM GREWALL

OUR TEAM OF INVISIBLE HELPERS
The Ones On the 'Other' Side

iUniverse books may be ordered through booksellers or by contacting:

iUniverse
1663 Liberty Drive
Bloomington, IN 47403
www.iuniverse.com
844-349-9409

Because of the dynamic nature of the Internet, any web addresses or links contained in this book may have changed since publication and may no longer be valid. The views expressed in this work are solely those of the author and do not necessarily reflect the views of the publisher, and the publisher hereby disclaims any responsibility for them.

Any people depicted in stock imagery provided by Getty Images are models, and such images are being used for illustrative purposes only.
Certain stock imagery © Getty Images.

ISBN: 978-1-6632-6476-3 (sc)
978-1-6632-6475-6 (hc)
978-1-6632-6474-9 (e)

Library of Congress Control Number: 2024914386

Print information available on the last page.

iUniverse rev. date: 07/19/2024

TABLE OF CONTENTS

PART I

INTRODUCTION

If I fill myself with all that you know, what room will I have left for all that you do not know?

- Khalil Gibran

When you read this book, it will be helpful to keep an open mind because you may find yourself out of your comfort zone with some parts of it while other parts of it may seem very familiar. Your acceptance of the information will depend on your current beliefs and how rigidly you hold them. While I make no claims to have all the answers, I am sharing what little I do know for those who are curious, have questions and are willing to learn from various sources.

You may also notice that I have stated the basic concepts several times in different words. I felt that this kind of repetition and emphasis on key points will help to reinforce the message.

You may find that there are some stories that are not about receiving help from the other side, but I felt these had valuable information, so I have included them also.

How this book came to be written is an interesting story. I had been working on my second book for a very long time. I had the first draft finally ready after many road blocks. However, as I started to edit that, I was told by my guides to change the format and topic altogether. While I had the free will to accept or reject the suggestion, I have found that things flow so much better when I listen to them so I made the change.

I was told that the purpose of this book is to help people learn and understand how invisible helpers on the other side work to teach, guide and help you and how you can invoke their help. It is important for people to be reminded of this as humanity transitions into the new world and things shift, because it may be a difficult and confusing period when many will feel lost unless you can recall what you all know at the soul level but very often forget in your human journey.

So, here I am with this topic and related stories for my book, while the previous draft will be used in another format when this is completed. As I switched gears, I started to see why this had to be changed. This is a format that will encourage self-study and self-reflection to provide a deeper understanding, which is the need of the hour. The previous topic will better serve as a dialogue or a conversation rather than a book.

This book includes stories that various people from different walks of life shared with me about how they have received help from unknown sources. They have been kind enough to give me permission to share their stories, because their vision of reaching out to those who may be struggling with difficult situations in their life aligned with mine. People who believe that others may take inspiration from knowing that they too have struggled, reached out to invoke help and have received help…to know that they are not alone. Some have chosen to remain anonymous, while others have shared their names and what they do. It will also help people to understand that 'no' is also a valid answer which is not necessarily a denial of help but an act of love, just as a parent might deny a child something that the child thinks is a toy but which the parent knows will hurt the child much more than the pain of being deprived of what the child is asking for.

Sometimes life seems like such a lonely experience where you feel totally lost and alone. Even with a multitude of people around you, you find yourself feeling lonely because it seems like no one understands your experience, no one has time to listen to your story and no one has any solution to your dilemma. This is where many are tempted to end it all and call it quits. You feel that your loved ones are busy living happy, productive, and fulfilling lives while you are struggling. You do not even attempt to reach out for help because you do not want to burst their bubble and drag them down into the depths of despair with you.

But is the reality of human existence really that bleak? Are you truly alone? The truth is that you are the creators of your own reality. As difficult as it is to believe, it is the truth. When a young child starts to go to daycare or school, he feels alone and afraid because he does not know anyone in this new environment. He may even feel abandoned. However, if he believes what his parents have told him and, in his heart, he knows that his parents would not just abandon him, he feels comfortable making new friends and playing with them. There are teachers in his school to take care of him. He knows that he is loved and taken care of. He knows that his parents will come and get him at the end of the day, or earlier if he needs them. The parents are just a phone call away!

In the same way, when you start your journey as human beings, it is like going to a daycare for the first time. Your parents are like the teachers in this place to take care of you and there is a team of 'helpers' on the other side where you came from. For those who believe or know, it is a source of comfort, just like the child who *knows* that his parents will be there to take him home at the end of the day.

While it is true that not everyone has such an idyllic experience in life, know that whatever challenging situations you may be facing in life, help from your team of invisible helpers is available to *everyone*!

About The Helpers

Your helpers, teachers and guides on the other side comprise 'your team.' They are always willing and able to help you even though very often you do not hear them or heed their advice because of your beliefs, fears, or lack of trust. It is important to build a relationship with your team of invisible helpers. The team may consist of your guardian angel, other angels, teachers, masters, people of your soul family and friends.

Each morning when you wake up, greet them. Since you may not know who all are there, it is okay to address them as 'my team' and acknowledge their presence. Then ask them to walk with you through the day and guide you to make better choices and decisions. Express gratitude for the help and guidance you have received. Thank them for what you asked for and received, but even more so, thank them for what you asked for but did not receive. Let them know that while you may not understand why a request was not answered, you realize that because they view life from a higher perspective, they know better and refusal just means that either what you asked for was not beneficial to you or they are sending something better. One such example is about when I was looking to purchase a mobile home. I found one, liked it and was ready to go ahead with the transaction. Well, there was a little problem. The previous owner was waiting for work to be completed on his condominium, where he planned to move, but there were many delays. The lease on my apartment was expiring, so I could not wait. Well, fast forward a year or so, and I was able to purchase my ideal home in a better neighborhood and with many more amenities. I was certainly grateful to 'my team' for not letting the mobile home sale go through!!

You may find that sometimes other specialists are called in who are not part of your regular team. Just as in large corporations, there is a dedicated team that oversees the smooth operation of various divisions, but periodically experts and consultants are called in for special projects. Your team is there to help you but may call on others with different abilities to join them if needed.

On a recent road trip, we were re-routed and found ourselves driving on snow covered roads through a totally deserted fifty-nine mile stretch with no people, animals, or buildings in sight. During that entire time, we saw only five cars, our phones were dying, the phone charger had died and we were running low on gas. I kept talking to my team and kept telling them that I accept where they were taking us even though it did not seem very safe or comfortable and I did not understand why we had been sent there. Well, soon after, we came upon a small convenience store in the middle of nowhere, that had a small gas station and phone chargers, just before everything would have come to a halt. Gratefully, we made it to the next town where we had decided to stay for the night because of the detour and had booked a hotel.

When we checked our phones the next day, we saw a few posts by people who were stuck on the road that we were supposed to take. There had been a thirty plus vehicle pile-up including several big trucks due to icy road conditions and everyone was stranded for hours. The team had certainly directed us to the lesser of two evils!!

Another example is about someone who found herself in a very dark place and could not seem to bring herself out of it. Her situation was getting worse by the day and family and friends rallied around, worried that she may harm herself. When I heard about it, I reached out to family and friends and had our guardian angels talk to her guardian angel, while calling on the rest of the team of loved ones on the other side to help her lift herself from this dark place. As they formed a protective circle around her and sent her the help that was needed, she was able to move past the dire situation. Everything did not suddenly become perfect, but she certainly was able to gain clarity and move forward in the right direction. She still needs to do a lot of work to ensure that she does not find herself in a similar situation again.

Recently, on "The Kelly Clarkson Show" there was a gentleman who gives hugs to people who may need them. Sometimes he even gives money if he senses that they may need it. One day he had been watching a traffic policewoman directing traffic and greeting everyone. He felt that she needed a hug but she could not stop what she was doing to receive the hug. He talked to her as she continued her work and decided to wait since her shift was ending in a few more minutes. Once she was off duty, she stepped aside to resume their conversation. He had a feeling that he should give her some money. He pulled out $500 from his pocket and offered it to her. She broke down and could not believe what was happening. Her son needed to pay his fees to join a certain class and was very disheartened because he did not have the funds and no hope of receiving any. His mother, the policewoman told him not to worry but to go ahead and apply anyway and then they both prayed for help. Neither of them had envisioned that this is how the help would arrive and just in time to deposit the fees!!!

In the guidebook for her set of Oracle Cards – Ask Your Guides, Sonia Choquette states that, "When it comes to asking for help from your guides, you don't need to follow fixed rules, but rather simply be sincere and direct, and of course be willing to accept the guidance they offer. (…) Your guides are willing to be supportive and to offer guidance as they show you how to create the best possible outcome in all situations and circumstances in your life. That's their job, and they love to be asked for help. So let them."

Believe it or not!

Unconditional love, guidance, and protection is always available to *all* human beings regardless of financial or spiritual status. In her book 'Great Minds Speak to You,' Tina Louise Spalding tells us that Spirit recognizes no higher or lower beings. You are all equal but since you vibrate on different speeds based on your light or dark, positive, or negative thoughts your vibration makes you appear dense or light, making you sink lower or float higher. Are you transparent, translucent, or opaque? Does your energy feel light or dark? The density of your vibration may affect your ability to see clearly or your hard held beliefs may prevent you from accepting the concept.

In order for you to really benefit from your divine gifts, make sure that:

➢ You love yourselves

➢ You know yourselves to be worthy of love

➢ You allow yourselves to be loved

➢ You learn how to ask for guidance and protection

➢ You ask for guidance and protection because you have free will! While your invisible guides and helpers are always willing and able to help you, you must ask for it, because they cannot impose their will upon your free will by stepping in unasked.

➢ You have accepted the unconditional love, and having asked for guidance and/or protection, you must now move out of your own way and open yourselves to receive it.

➢ You pray with the faith of a child and believe that your prayers will be answered regardless of whether the answer is 'yes' or 'no.' If you doubt or think that 'Oh, I know I am not going to get it but I will ask anyway,' you are already closing the door. This reminds me of the story where the entire village gathered to pray for rain, but only one small child showed up with an umbrella!

➤ You should be aware and recognize when help is received unlike the person who was stranded on a tree due to a flash flood, praying for help. Three boats came by and offered to help him but he refused saying that he was waiting for God to help him since he had prayed to Him for help. He was eventually swept away in the rising water and died. When he saw God, he complained and asked why he was not helped when he had prayed for help. God replied that He had sent three boats, but the man had refused that help because he was looking for it to arrive in a way that he thought it should, instead of accepting it as it was sent in answer to his prayers.

➤ Finally, you express gratitude! Be grateful even if the answer is 'no.' You will find that eventually you will receive something better. Since spirit responds from a higher perspective than your limited ego-based one, it knows that some things that you ask for may not be good for you in the long run or to receive it at this time, so it holds off to send something better or at a time when it would serve you better.

Believe that your prayer will be answered.
Have *Faith* that your prayer will be answered in the best way.
Know that what you prayed for or something better is coming to you.

More evidence of the magical workings of the universe can be found all around you if you only open your eyes and look carefully. The skeptics will discount any evidence but the believers will need no proof. Have you received any help through a gut feeling or a timely prompting in your mind that you have called 'just a coincidence?' You as consciousness evolve to higher levels, because you learn new information about higher dimensions. Souls on their journeys before you have done that and there will be many more who will follow and do the same. Right now, it is your time to scan the landscape and walk through doors that are opening for you. When you are ready to receive this knowledge, answers may come in the form of someone speaking to you, or you could overhear a random conversation or find a book that answers the questions in your minds or some other way.

When I first came to USA from India, I would talk quite normally about reincarnation, a concept that is accepted readily in India, but in USA, I found myself encountering uncomfortable silences or people staring at me in disbelief. I then realized that for my western friends it was an alien concept that they had either not heard of or did not believe in. I then prayed to find a way to talk about this eastern philosophy comfortably to a western audience.

One day, I had to take my children to the library to check out books for class projects they were working on. As they went about looking for the books they needed, I decided to look for my next read in the Metaphysical/Spiritual section. Suddenly a book literally fell on my head from the top shelf. I picked it up to put it back on the shelf when I realized it was a book about reincarnation by Ruth Montgomery, a writer I had never heard of. Well, this gave me an insight into information that a western audience would relate to although there are non-believers both in the east and the west.

Quite often, you do not recognize the significance of a chance encounter or a random conversation. For example, I had gone to Rita's farm to pick up some eggs. I met Rita when I was buying raw milk from a lady who came to a place near my home once a week. Rita also got raw milk while she brought eggs from her farm to sell. So, it was a two-in-one stop for me. Tammy had to discontinue these weekly visits to our neighborhood for personal reasons. While we could still get milk from her farm, it was too far for me to make the trip every week. In the meantime, I found another source.

I had not seen Rita in a long while due to life happening, as it often does. So, when I was able to stop by, I was hoping to see her, instead of just picking up the eggs from the designated place and leaving the money there. I did not see her, but as I was walking back to my car, I heard her call out to me. We stopped to have a little chat and catch up on what was going on in our lives. I asked her if she had found another source for raw milk, which she said she had not. I then told her about where I was getting it, in case she was interested. She said that she was okay not getting the milk.

Well, an hour or so later, I got a text from her asking me about contact information of the person selling the raw milk. Another lady, who also purchased eggs from her had stopped by after I left and just randomly asked her if she knew of anyone selling raw milk!!!

Life on earth as humans is no party. When spirit chooses to incarnate as a human being on the 'school' planet aka Mother Earth, it takes on a body which it uses as a vehicle on its journey. To facilitate the learning, spirit must limit its unlimited capabilities and subject itself to the required discipline, just as students curb the freedom they have at home while they are in school. Just as there are adults who hold various positions in the school system to facilitate the process and for efficient working of the system to teach, guide, discipline, and direct their activities, there are teachers and guides who help us from the other side. While the students have freedom to choose the courses they want to study, once the selection is made, they are required to attend classes to study those subjects so they can take an exam to have their learning assessed. In the end it is all about gaining knowledge and experience. Similarly, you choose experiences for your journey that will teach you what you need to learn. Now it is up to you whether you learn from them or lose yourselves in the pleasures of your physical life only or become bitter because of the painful experiences. Not everyone who registers for classes will graduate. As Antonio Sangio shares a quote in his book 'Guiding Lost Souls:'

(…) *although you spirits come with a defined learning plan or with specific functions and missions, this does not guarantee a successful outcome.*

Enjoy life without becoming too attached to the material goods or going to the other extreme of denying yourself altogether for fear of becoming too attached. It is like enjoying a swim in the water without ingesting the water that will make you drown or staying out of the water altogether for fear of drowning.

As I look back on so many events in my life, I find that without consciously realizing, I had been communing with my support 'team' on the other side. – way before I learned how it works or who all make up that team.

So, who all do make up this team that you can call on?

The team can be made up of all or some of the Masters, guides, teachers, angels, family, and friends, who come together to lend you support when and as you need it depending on the area that you may seek help in. Of course, as stated before, you must ask for it – and having asked, you should move out of your own way to not block that support when it comes through. Do not tell them how you want to receive it or set a time limit. Those demands are ego based and come from a limited perspective, unlike receiving an answer from a higher perspective. I have learned that when you set aside your ego, (which you do not need to eliminate or kill altogether since you need it to function in this world) but do not put it in the driver's seat, life works magically. Doing that will assure you that help will arrive just when you need it and, in a way, that is much better than you could have ever imagined.

There have been so many other incidents in my life where I have received timely help and guidance. I have shared a few of these in my book 'How to Help Yourself to Be Who You Want to Be.' At a very low point in my life, I had prayed for help and I received that help in a most dramatic way. No, I did not recognize it right away and even questioned it, but eventually I could not deny it.

In the second part of this book, I share many more of my stories and some very magical ones from people from all around the globe who work in different fields. You can decide if you think these stories are proof that you have a team of helpers or if you think these are merely coincidences that just happened that way?

Most people have heard of angels and are familiar with the benevolent nature of the winged ones, while others only know of them as cherubs that they have seen on TV or read about in books. Many do not believe in them but consider them a figment of people's imagination.

Truth is that angels do exist and their only job is to help, support and guide human beings in dealing with difficult situations that you may face in your lives. You were not sent on earth alone. In fact, each one of you have your very own guardian angel who is always with you. In addition, you can call on various other sources as mentioned above.

The 'team' is always ready to help you, answer your prayers and fulfil your requests if these are within the parameters of certain guidelines.

Let us recap…

➢ Because you have free will, you must ask for help. They cannot step in on their own and take over.

➢ You must ask not from your ego but from a higher perspective, for example, you can ask for joyful experiences or even material goods if they fulfil your need and not just serve your greed.

➢ You should acknowledge their presence, state your request politely with the faith that they are listening and will fulfill them. You certainly should not make demands or dictate how and when they should do their work! Keep in mind that 'no' is also a valid answer. Just as a parent you frequently say 'no' to your child because you know that what they are asking for is not good for them or will hurt them. Your team also knows much more than you do because they view your situation from a higher perspective since they are not limited by a physical body. You can be sure that if you have not received what you asked for, it is because having it would not have been good for you or would have hurt you in some way or that something better is coming your way if you just wait a little longer.

➢ Be sure to express gratitude for their presence in your life, especially when you receive what you asked for or even when you did not receive it. Gratitude expressed and appreciation stated opens many more doors and strengthens the bond. If you are always unhappy and complaining, it closes the channels to your heart. By replacing these with joy and gratitude, you can expand the love in your heart and re-open the channels to receive.

Does this sound like a fairy tale? Well, it sure works magically if you follow the rules and ask within the guidelines. After all life is a game, rules are important and cheating disqualifies you.

A lot of this information was prompted by Spirit/guides and invisible team of helpers such as how information or events are processed and why you remember some more vividly than others and as if they are happening now instead of years ago.

Is prayer a way of asking for help? Is prayer only an expression of gratitude? Do you know what purpose prayers and rituals serve? Do you have to pray only in a designated place of worship or in a certain way? Of course not! While all that serves a purpose, prayer can be as formal or informal as you choose as long as it is respectful and spoken from the heart.

Prayer is a powerful tool if performed from the heart and not merely recited. Although formal prayer is not essential, sometimes it works better. When you say your prayers in a formal manner, you tend to be more focused, so you can express your wishes more clearly. However, if you are in a place of worship and are just repeating a written formal text while your mind is wandering elsewhere, the power of the prayer will be diluted and not convey clear intention. There is a big difference between expressing the love you feel and merely acting out a love scene. Just as memorizing a formula without understanding how it works may or may not really help you, a verse from the scriptures memorized and recited without understanding or feeling any connection will not move you. Prayers have immense power when performed with a knowledge of and an understanding of the symbolism behind them. Emotions are the energy source that power the words and express feelings. Thoughts work behind the scenes and are great in manifesting what people create in their lives. Very often the problem is that the words spoken are different from the feelings they want to express because most people do not want others to really know what they want or how they feel, so they hide behind the invisible walls they put up. Your helpers listen to your thoughts and feelings rather than to empty words that are disconnected from the real you.

Another practice that has become meaningless is the performance of rituals that were meaningful at some point in the past but have lost their relevance now because not only have the basics changed but the performers neither know the origin of nor understand the significance of the rituals they are now performing. Having lost that connection, it makes the rituals empty and ineffective. While they appease the need of human nature for pageantry, they no longer help to gain a deeper comprehension of the spiritual selves aka their God nature.

Human beings now go through the motions but only because this is what has been done for generations even though they do not understand why it is done like that. Their meaning and essence are lost over generations because the 'why' and 'what' behind the physical performance is forgotten, making it incomplete and incapable of engaging the higher self or the whole self. Just as a human being is incapacitated by losing a limb, the rituals become mere physical performances without the understanding of the significance and the reason for the actions, thus reducing their impact. They are like a body from which spirit has left – they are dead and unable to be the source of knowledge and understanding of the purpose for which they were originally created. This disconnection then makes people feel like victims over time because even though they continue to perform the actions just because 'this is how it has been done for generations' they no longer remember why they are doing it.

Praying for others is a noble gesture if you keep in mind that when praying to invoke help for someone else, you should be sure not to take on their problems. It is important to do so as an observer only and not to identify too closely with the person or their problems. This does not imply that you do not care, just that you respect their free will and are not imposing your wishes, thoughts, and beliefs on them because you think you are doing them a favor. Remember, as much as you want to help, they have free choice too which you should not encroach upon. If you do that, not only is it not helping them but you are interfering with their learning. These tough situations are meant to help them learn the lessons that they need to. By taking on what they need to experience, you let them continue to feel like victims and encourage self-pity besides facilitating and justifying their staying in the same place rather than moving forward. You cannot live anyone else's life for them. There is a lesson here for you too. Extend a helping hand when someone trips and falls so they can regain their balance and get back on their feet but do not become their crutch. By helping like this, you become stronger and wiser since you extend the same opportunity to others.

Being compassionate does not mean pitying them. Offering support should not mean depriving them of their choices. By continuing to learn your lessons and living your lives with better choices, you can become examples that they can learn from and follow. You are all part of One Consciousness. You help others even as you help yourselves.

It is amazing how information may be received through books suggested by others or through videos randomly popping up or even through conversations. While collecting stories for my second book, one of the contributors suggested a book that she found very interesting. Of course, it fit in with what I was writing about and I now share that information with my readers. The book is titled 'Great Minds Speak to You' by Tina Louise Spalding. It is a compilation of messages channeled from various celebrities and other famous people, sharing their experiences, knowledge, and wisdom about life after what you know as death and how you receive help and guidance from experts in the field, provided you keep your channels open to receive such help.

Now who is directing you to the answers you are seeking? Your own team of helpers is always available to bring you the information you seek. As mentioned above, this information can be brought to your attention through various means.

Do you know who all make up your team of helpers?

Your team can include any or all the following in addition to your own guardian angel:

➢ Your higher self or God self

➢ More advanced souls

➢ Angels

➢ Teachers and Masters

➢ Family and friends

Help is always available to everyone. When you ask sincerely, directly and with love, your request is heard more clearly and moves powerfully. It is even more effective if your needs, wants, and intentions are stated clearly without setting a time limit or directing them on how to manifest those for you.

Another very important thing to keep in mind is that the universe hears your message in a very precise language of what you want rather than of what you do not want. For example, say I want to be rich…rather than saying I do not want to be poor…because 'no' or 'not' is not heard since it is perceived as an expressed wish. This is the power of the spoken word. If you only realized the full power of the spoken word, you would be more cautious of the words you use.

Having done that, you need to make sure that you have opened yourselves to receive it instead of blocking it with doubt or other negative thoughts. Believe that you will receive what you ask for at the right time and in the right way. If you focus so much on how you expect it to show up, you will miss it when it does come through.

Understand that 'no' is also a valid answer. If you do not receive what you asked for, it could be because what you asked for is not good for you or something better is on its way. A story about this was shared in my book 'How to Help Yourself to Be Who You Want to Be.' My father had stopped praying because he was upset with his Heavenly Father since he did not get what he had asked for. A holy man was visiting the family and he asked my father whether he prayed. Dad told him that now he did not do so, since he was upset with God, whom he considered as his Heavenly Father because he had not received what he had asked for. Before the holy man could make a comment on that statement, my brother who was a toddler then, came into the room and grabbed the knife that was on the table to cut fruit. My father took away the knife from my brother and of course he started crying. The holy man asked my father to give the child the knife since he was crying. My father looked shocked and said that the child would stop crying in a little bit, but he could injure himself badly with the knife. The holy man smiled benevolently and stated that this was exactly what he was trying to explain. Your Heavenly Father is so much wiser than you, the earthly father, so He knows that you will cry for a while, but if He gives you what you want, it would hurt you more.

Gratitude for what you receive or do not receive should also be expressed frequently because it lets your team know that you appreciate their help. Knowing that, they respond more promptly. It is not that they are looking for your gratitude or your appreciation, but when you express it, they know that you are pleased and it gives you happiness, so it is a good thing for you.

Another factor in receiving or not receiving what you ask for is karma. Karma is simply the law of having you experience what you chose to make others experience. For example, if you swindled someone of their hard-earned money in a previous life and that person died in poverty, struggling to make ends meet, in this life you may be experiencing poverty by being swindled, to learn how it felt. So, if you ask to be rich now, you will probably not receive it. Karma keeps us repeating similar patterns but you can break that cycle by forgiving the person who hurt you. You should also forgive yourself for what you may have done to propagate this cycle. Forgiving someone for their transgression does not imply that it did not happen or that it did not hurt. It simply means that you recognize that the other person made a choice that he is responsible for and took action that he is accountable for, but you are now choosing to not be a part of that equation any more. You separate yourself from this situation by understanding that he has free will, just as you do, and while he may be making choices from a lack of understanding, you are choosing not to be aligned to that negative energy any more.

One of my many mentors and teachers, Gary Quinn shares his experience about receiving help from Archangel Michael in his book, 'May The Angels Be With You'. While pursuing his music career, he had moved to Paris after signing a contract for various performances in France. Unfortunately, when he got there, he found that the contract had been cancelled due to unforeseen circumstances and now he was stranded there with no place to stay, no work and very little money. Coming back was not a viable option since he had sold everything. He had to move forward, but how? He decided to go to Notre Dame to pray and to seek guidance and help. While there, archangel Michael appeared before him with a message, so he felt comforted and knew that somehow all would be well. He was still encompassed in the warmth of that experience when he got back to his hotel. Suddenly, his phone rang. It was a friend who needed to travel to USA and wanted Gary to house sit for him for a couple months. Well, now that living arrangements had fallen in place and he was able to earn some money while doing that, he had time to figure out his next step!

Life works in mysterious ways. It can be confusing and overwhelming, especially if you are too busy 'doing' and rushing instead of 'being' and living. In your haste you tend to misread the signs and misinterpret the messages received. When your helpers and guides send you subtle messages through your thoughts, gut feelings or even that voice in your head, you can only understand it based on your frame of reference, limited by your scope of knowledge. Here is a perfect example of how people can only comprehend the truth based on what they know or believe.

He had come to USA from India, and one of the first jobs he had, was cleaning chickens at a Foster Farms facility. Never having had to work in India, he found the work tough and tedious and the hours long. His nails took a toll from cleaning countless chickens. He worked there long enough to save enough money to buy an airplane ticket so he could go back home for a visit before looking for another job.

When he got home, his family and friends rushed to meet him and hear stories of his adventures in America. They were very shocked to see the sorry state of his nails and questioned him about it. He explained that in the factory where he worked, they cleaned millions of chickens per day. Many of them refused to believe the explanation and thought he was spinning a yarn to fool them. They did not believe that as big as it was, even all of America could consume that many chickens. He could not dispel their disbelief, so he just told them that when he was in the plane, he had opened the window and it slammed down on his hands. Of course, they believed this. After all, how many of them had smashed their hands while trying to close the windows on a bus or a train so it could easily have happened in the plane.

Similarly, when you are presented with the idea of having guides, teachers and helpers on the other side who are always there to help you when you ask, people accept only what fits in with their beliefs or falls within the scope of their study.

Understanding this concept and making it work for you requires a lot of knowledge, wisdom, and comprehension.

For example, while the internet is a blessing that brings knowledge from around the world and places it at your fingertips, just as much fake information and angry comments circulate on it. For the discerning mind it is an excellent tool but for an indiscriminating one, it can be like a maze that keeps one lost and in confusion.

To benefit from it and use it as a source of knowledge and a valuable resource, first connect with yourself, so you are not merely surfing the surface of the 'ocean' but are prepared to dive deeper and pick the pearls of wisdom. When you have learned to choose wisely and separate the core from the fluff, you are able to differentiate between the good and the bad, the useful and the useless and everything in between. You can separate truth from lies, light from dark. You learn to pick your battles because you realize that you do not have to engage in every controversy.

Another analogy that may help you to gain a greater understanding is about towns and cities which already exist but you become aware of their energy only as you travel through them. Similarly, life is always there all the time, but you relate events to it as you focus on what is happening in the 'now' because you experience it sequentially.

Let us say that you travel from Point A to Point B, and stop on the way at Point A1, you are no longer at Point A (past) and not yet at Point B (future). Point A1 is your present and that is where you are now physically present. It is important that you also be there mentally, emotionally, and spiritually to enjoy the complete experience. Being sad because you are no longer at Point A or anxious because you are not yet at Point B, will rob you of the ability to enjoy the present moment at Point A1

Most people only focus on their human nature and what can be seen and felt while completely ignoring their 'God-Self' because they have chosen to separate it from themselves and have created a Higher Power that is separate from themselves. They do not believe that everything is connected in the universe and that this Higher Power is a part of them. While the smallest cell functions independently, it connects with other cells to form the total human being. Our human nature/ego marks the separation lines for the journey of our human experience and learning, and the Spirit that we are, keeps us connected to Source/Higher Powers/ our God-self.

With that knowledge, you can understand how it benefits you to put your God-Self in the driver's seat and let your human nature be guided by it. But again, like an errant child who wants to do everything for himself, our human nature does not wish to be subservient to anyone. It does not realize how much more he can be empowered with the guidance and learning from its God-Self. That is one more lesson it will learn in the school of life.

Learning encompasses gathering knowledge, gaining wisdom, and acting, based on that. At each step it is important to reflect and assess your growth and the path you are choosing lest you lose yourself in the chaos. It is easy to get lost in the knowledge and be overwhelmed by the sheer volume of it.

To know, understand, comprehend, and act are four separate steps.

Even though you know something because you have read about it or learned about it, you gain wisdom only when you really understand it.

For example –

Knowledge – You should think positive thoughts.

Wisdom – You understand what positive thoughts are. You understand the benefits of positive thoughts, and you comprehend the importance of positive thoughts.

Action – You act on that and practice thinking positive thoughts and replacing negative thoughts as they occur.

Beware the ego that is always ready to step in. When you gather knowledge, it is easy to inflate the ego because you 'know so much!' Another thing to keep in mind is that after you have gathered all this knowledge, unless you act upon that knowledge in your wisdom, you are simply a storage facility for it. You have not gained wisdom just because you know something. There is a lot of knowledge stored in the computer, but it cannot take any action on it or use it in any meaningful way. It is simply a storehouse of knowledge. If you do the same and merely 'know' then you are not using your full faculties and are no different from the computer.

Computer is a man-made machine. You are a lot more complex. The computer is created in your image. Dr. Gregg Braden says that any kind of technology that you see today is inspired by the technology that you are. You do not always understand the full scope of your being. You do not comprehend your potential and capabilities because the sophisticated technology that you are does not come with an instruction manual. To really understand yourselves and know your full potential, you must spend time with yourselves and know yourselves at a much deeper level. This requires self-reflection, something many of us fear for a variety of reasons. However, once you recognize the sophisticated instruments that you are and deeply comprehend it, you will then elevate yourselves from being merely knowledgeable to being wise.

Now how do you act on that knowledge and wisdom? How do you utilize your resources? Do you realize that you are a part of God/Universe/Source or whatever other name you choose to call it? You are spirit, until you incarnate into a physical body. Then you are soul and you are equipped with an ego that helps you to navigate through the school of life and have your individual experiences on earth. Here, in your wisdom you understand the interconnectedness of the entire creation even though your ego defines separation lines between everyone. You are like cells in the 'body' of God, just like a body is made up of many cells that multiply, grow, and create your physical selves. You know that you need to nourish the cells, to take care of your body at the cellular level because you understand that this is the vehicle that facilitates your journey of learning. You know the purpose that having a body serves, and you understand why you need to take care of it by providing it the right nutrition. Do you, despite knowing and understanding just eat what only tastes good, instead of what is also good for you even though it may not always taste that good? This is where you need to learn to work with yourself because although your brain understands and comprehends, your mind often leads you with stories of how you are a victim of circumstances and that things happen to you that you have no control over. Your brain knows that you are in charge. In your wisdom, you need to act accordingly. You choose your experiences that will facilitate the lessons you need to learn. Even though you do not remember doing so, you are soul and spirit who has chosen to take on the physical body for the experiences that will teach you faster than staying in the world of spirit would have done, just as attending school teaches you so many more skills than what you would learn by just staying at home. No matter how many books you read on a subject, unless you experience it yourself, you will not truly understand and learn from it. For example, simply hearing about or reading about childbirth will not give you the experience. Linked to the pain of that experience is also the experience of an intense love for the child and wonder of the human being you have created. Added to that are the highs, lows, joys, sorrows, rewards, and frustration of raising those children. Not everyone experiences the same emotions with a similar intensity which is because of the person's physical, mental, and emotional health. It is all connected and inter-dependent.

When my children were growing up, I would always say to them – May the angels guard and guide you. It was just something that had popped up in my head, so I said it. I did not think too much about it and did not try to tell the angels how I wanted them to guard and guide my children.

I cannot even count how many times I arrived 'just in time' to prevent a disaster that I was not even aware was happening at home. Or when I got to know that they were up to some mischief. I was not always aware of some silly things that they were doing or safely experimenting with life – but if it was something that would lead them astray or on a path of no return, it was brought to my attention by something they would say or something that I'd find or overhear. I did not invade their privacy but if I was made aware of some such incident, I did check it out.

That was not the only help I received. There were other more dramatic instances!

Once when I was having financial difficulties, I had pleaded for help and a lady had been sent to help me. I have shared this and some other similar incidents in my book, 'How to Help Yourself to Be Who You Want to Be'. (www.pamgrewall.com). There are many more stories that I share in this book now.

It has become quite normal for me to voice what I want or need and soon after, I will find myself randomly in a place where I find the exact thing I asked for.

I always express gratitude for what I receive and even for what I do not receive. I have learned that if I did not receive what I asked for – either it was because it would not have been good for me or I have received something better instead.

➢ And that my friends is the secret to enhancing your life experiences.

To recap –

➢ Ask clearly

➢ Move out of your own way so you can receive it

➢ Express gratitude when you receive it

➢ Express gratitude even if you do not receive it, because sooner or later you will learn that some disaster was averted by that refusal or that the something else which you received instead is so much better.

'More things are wrought by prayer than the world dreams of.' - Unknown

Reflect on this…*Did my thoughts manifest me or do I create my thoughts?*

Sometimes you are guided to something that you need to know or learn for your life's purpose. This is not something you may have asked for consciously but it may be the purpose you chose to fulfil before coming in to this life. It is easy to get lost in the myriad things that happen, so spirit gently prompts you with reminders and brings helpful knowledge for you to pay attention to.

Years ago, I subscribed to a magazine called 'New Woman.' In one of the issues, there was a write up about a book called 'Out on A Limb' by Shirley McLaine. I looked at it and thought to myself…here's another celebrity writing her life story and I refused to read it. My guides had other ideas though. Each time I opened the magazine, it would open to that page. I argued with myself and shut it every time. A few days later, I went to visit a friend. As I walked in, I saw the book on her coffee table. Well, I asked her what she thought of it. She picked it up, handed it to me and said that she could not really connect with it, so would I please read it and tell her about it!! So, I did! It was amazing to find that as I read through the book, I felt like I was reading my own thoughts on paper written by someone else. Now years later, I realize that I was meant to write a book, but I had let myself get overwhelmed with living up to everyone else's expectations and not taken the time to be focused on what I needed to do.

Well, the magic did not end there. My cousin told me that a TV movie was being produced based on the book. I did not know when it would air to set the VCR to record it. With my work and children's schedules, I did not think it would work. One day, at our retail store, business was slow on a weekday, so my husband told me I could go home early since the weekend would be very busy. Guess what? I came home just in time to watch 'The Oprah Winfrey Show' with her guest Shirley Mclaine talking about the movie and when it would air!!!

Part II

Stories

I feel that I am so connected to my spirit that I can call on my 'team' for help and it becomes readily available. When I look back on my life, I see so many incidents of when I asked and received help although I did not see that clearly at the time.

I have also shared many stories about receiving timely help and guidance from many individuals who have been gracious enough to give me permission to do so. Some wished to remain anonymous, but others have come forth as they all support this premise with their experiences. Due to their experiences, many have chosen to work in spiritual modalities to help others who may be struggling in their lives. All of them believe in their spiritual connections despite having been raised with different religious beliefs. Some could recall only one instance where they felt there was divine assistance, others see many such occurrences in their lives. The point I am trying to make is that one does not have to work in any esoteric field or be spiritually aware to receive help. When a person sends up a prayer for protection or guidance or for any number of reasons, specific teams are directed to answer those prayers. Prayers are not always verses recited from various scriptures, but are often heartfelt pleas for assistance. When your heart is involved in the asking and the asking is done lovingly, strong emotions propel it forward to Source and then action is set in motion. Other times it could simply be your guardian angel that may see some danger and then redirect your path in some way for you to avoid that danger. How many times have you heard stories of plane crashes where people who were supposed to be on certain flights missed those for some reason or their plans changed. Does that mean that the people who died in those flights did not get help? No, it simply means that it was their chosen time and method of completing their journey in this incarnation.

Sometimes help is received without asking because you are not even aware of the danger that lies ahead of you. Other times, when you are in a tight spot or caught up in a storm and are not able to see your way out of your dilemma, you send out the request. You may have heard some people complain that they asked for help but did not receive it. Did you consider that it could be that you had not opened yourself to receive the help that was sent or you were so busy looking for it to come through in that one way that you knew in your limited wisdom, that you did not see how it actually came through and you missed it?

The following stories were shared with me in the hope that they may help someone to see light when they are struggling in darkness, and inspire them to follow that ray of light to lift them out of the depths of despair. These also indicate that one does not need to belong to any particular religion or be particularly spiritual or have any special understanding of how it works. All you need to do is ask, even hesitantly, kind of hoping someone is listening and then move out of your own way, somewhat believing that you will receive that help. When I say move out of your own way, I mean do not demand that it be answered in a certain way at a certain time. Universe responds in its own time for best outcome and you will be surprised to find that when things do not work out as you hoped or wanted, it was either because that outcome would not have been good for you or that something better was sent your way.

TIMELY WARNING!

He remembers this very clearly! He was about nine years old. He and his family were travelling through the desert. The road was empty for miles and there was nothing but sand all around. His father was driving or you could truthfully say that he was flying too low…taking advantage of the empty road to give his boys a little thrill of speed.

Suddenly in the distance they saw two dogs just standing in the middle of the road. His father wondered aloud about where the dogs came from and what they were doing in the middle of the road. To assess the situation as they neared the spot where the dogs were standing, his father slowed down considerably and went around to avoid hitting them. As his father did so, he saw that there was a big pothole there. If his father had not slowed down and continued at the speed they were going, they would surely have flown off the road and most likely they would all have been killed since in those days there were no seat belts in the cars.

Although he never figured out where those dogs had come from since there were no dwellings or any people visible nearby, he felt very certain that some force had sent the dogs to get their attention so they could avoid an impending disaster.

MY AWESOME ANGEL

My sister absolutely loved to dance with her husband! Unfortunately, he passed away while she still had many dance steps left in her. She resolved her dilemma creatively by taking private ballroom dance lessons and entering competitions. Over the years, she even won many gold medals. I was so proud of her efforts, diligence and dedication and was happy to offer transportation service!

My story begins during one of these occasions while I was transporting her home from a dance competition. She looked beautiful sitting in the passenger seat with her hair and make-up tastefully done by a professional. It still looked perfect despite the long day and after performing various dances in the competition. She was very excited about her performance and was regaling me with stories about the dances she competed in, the ones she enjoyed and the ones she did not enjoy. She also told me how she thought her performance went.

Even though I was listening to her, I had to focus on my driving, since we were stuck in rush hour traffic. I was in the curb lane while a big truck was in the middle lane making a left turn. A young man driving from the opposite direction was also making a left turn at the intersection. Since the truck was blocking his view of the curb lane where my car was, he did not see my car. Instead of proceeding cautiously due to the blocked view and limited visibility, he drove right through even though I had the right of way. When I saw his car, it was perpendicular to mine and there was no time to stop. I tried to stop! I stood on the brake! I clenched the steering wheel and willed myself to stop!

I did stop when my car T-boned his car bringing us both to a halt. The air bags went off and the car filled with smoke, apparently from the air bags. I did not know at the time that that is what happens when air bags go off. I thought the car was on fire. I yelled at my sister to get out of the car which she promptly did and then I too got out of my car. I immediately realized that I could not stand because there was no feeling where my legs were supposed to be. My first thought was that my legs were cut off. Horrified at the possibility, I quickly looked down and was relieved to see my legs still connected to my body. Then I looked for blood to be gushing from some deep wound forming a puddle at my feet. All was well…or so I thought until I noticed my legs were rapidly expanding and trying to tear through my jeans! Using my car for support, I was able to walk curb side to where an older woman was standing with a chair. She helped me sit down and instructed me to just relax. Once the shock wore off, she asked me if I thought I could walk to a spot where her tree offered shade from the grueling summer sun. She then left and came back with two glasses of water for my sister and me. She stayed with us until my husband arrived and took us both to the hospital. Although nothing was broken, the soft tissue from my knees down was destroyed. To this day I still have that problem with my legs. My sister received a scratch on her eye from the debris inside the air bags that blew up on impact. Fortunately, that did heal.

Fast forward four months to Christmas. I was remembering the accident and thinking what an awesome angel that woman was during my time of need. Oh, and in the chaotic and emotional turmoil, I did not even thank her! In the Christmas spirit, I decided to rectify that and buy her a Christmas present. Knowing nothing more than where she lived, which is a very poor neighborhood, I decided to give her a gift certificate from the local grocery store. On the way to her house, I decided that if she needed transportation to and from the grocery store, I would take care of that too. This was turning into an exciting adventure for me. When I got to her house, I was surprised and confused to see that it was deserted. It looked like nobody had lived there for years! The yard was filled with debris and overgrown weeds. Ah! I recalled that she had gone in through the back door to get water for me and my sister, so I decided to check out the back door. There was so much decaying rubbish in the back, that I could not even get close to the door. I managed to push through the debris to a broken side window. The place was full of junk and reeked of rotting decay. It was obvious that nobody had lived there for years. I did not know what to think and I did not see anyone around who could answer my questions!

When I got home, I looked up the house in the county records, only to find it has been owned by an LLC for over five years. This confirmed my suspicions.

During my time of need, God sent an awesome angel to take care of me. I knelt and thanked God and my awesome angel. The gift certificate went into the church collection plate. I believe God orchestrated the delivery of that gift certificate to a family in need during the Christmas holiday.

An Angel to Comfort Me

My father was in the hospital. He was very ill and while we knew that he was not going to make it out, we were still in denial and not ready to let go. I was sitting by his bed, almost hoping that if I did not leave his side, he would not go. Suddenly I was shaken out of my reverie when a gentleman walked in, introduced himself as my father's friend and proceeded to comfort me by gently reminding me that death is a part of life and my father's ill health was keeping him in pain with poor quality of life. He also suggested that I should say a prayer for him and release him instead of holding on, because he was ready to go. Then he proceeded to walk me out of the room and told me to go home while he sat by his friend. When I got home, I asked Mom about this 'uncle' whom I had never seen before even though he claimed to be dad's friend. My mother had no idea who it could be. The description I gave did not fit any friend that she knew. I did not know his name since he had only introduced himself as my dad's friend and not given a name. No one at the hospital seemed to know where he had come from or where he went.

I wholeheartedly believe that it was an angel who had come to comfort and guide me to go out of the room so my dad could depart and find his peace.

My first marriage had fallen apart a few years before my dad's illness. My ex-husband had taken our son away. Even though I tried to meet my son at designated places and within court ordered meeting places, those were never honored by his father. I did go to court for his custody, but in those days the custody of boys went to the father after the age of seven. His father dragged the case until my son turned seven and then I was totally out of his life.

I was trying to move forward with my life. I had met someone else and we were ready to get married. By now dad had been unwell for some time. He was in the hospital. Even though none of us were ready to say goodbye to him, he finally succumbed in June 1988. It was a difficult farewell since I was very close to him.

In India we celebrate a festival called Rakhi or Raksha Bandhan, meaning a 'bond of protection' where women tie a string on the wrist of their brothers as a reminder to seek their protection, and the brothers give them a gift in return as acknowledgement of that honor. Although in recent times it is usually tied on a brother's wrist, in olden days, it was tied on a father's or even husband's wrist…basically the male members of the family. I used to tie a rakhi on my father's wrist also and he would always give me a gift or cash to buy myself a gift.

In Feb 1989, I got married again. That year Rakhi Festival fell in late July. It is on a different day each year, since most festivals follow a Lunar calendar instead of the universally accepted Solar calendar. I missed my dad terribly as I remembered that I could no longer tie the rakhi. In my mind and my heart, I said a prayer and asked for his blessing. That night, my mother had a dream. In her dream she saw my dad and he told her that he had already given me a gift for rakhi.

It was soon after that I found out I was pregnant. My daughter was conceived then and she was born in March, 1990.

I have always felt that my dad blessed me with a beautiful child, as he was aware of how much I was still hurting from my first born having been taken away from me. I frequently see dad in my dreams and although he does not talk, I feel his presence around me and I feel that he is my guardian angel.

THE FINAL GOODBYE

L ife was good! I was based in Bahrain for my work and loved both – Bahrain and my work. I was in love and in a relationship with the man I loved! What could be better?

Matt and I seemed to have a soul connection!

Unfortunately, life does not always work out as you wish and hope. When or why things changed, I really cannot pinpoint. The reason for our breakup was bizarre but it happened. I moved back to India and moved on with my life. After settling down and finding my bearings again, I met someone and started dating again. I was still hurting from my broken connection with Matt, who I thought was the love of my life and my soul mate.

Brandon, the new man in my life was easy to talk to, he was open to listening and emotionally supportive. I found myself pouring my heart out and telling him about how confused and hurt I was about my breakup with Matt despite our deep connection.

One day Brandon and I decided to venture out of town along with my best friend for an event. I was excited about attending the event and had looked forward to having a good time in good company, so I could not understand why I was feeling so uneasy. At one point I even started crying and started speaking to Matt, whose vision was crystal clear in my head. When we got back home, I went to check my email and saw that there was a notification of an email from Matt. It had been a long gap of no communication - neither seeing nor talking to each other. I asked Brandon if it would be okay for me to check my email account that Matt and I shared but which I had not accessed since our breakup. In that account I had received an email from his family. This was strange! Why would his family be accessing his account to contact me? To this day I wish I had not opened it although in a way I am glad I did otherwise I would have always wondered and never known…

Matt was declared dead the day that I had seen his vision and heard him speak to me.

It seems he had come to say his final goodbye to me.

THE OWL CONNECTION

I seem to have an inexplicable connection with Owls. One morning, I woke up to find an owl sitting on my leg! While by itself it would be an unusual occurrence, in a crowded city like Mumbai, it was even more strange that it was inside my house and sitting on my leg.

Since that day, I am either following owls or being followed by them. Regardless of where I travel, I see them everywhere. There is even an owl family that has built a nest right outside my window. They sit on my car or in my parking spot. Occasionally they dive down outside my window almost as if they are trying to get my attention and saying hello. At first it felt very weird seeing them everywhere I went, but now I have accepted them as my spirit bird. I feel very comforted when I see them around. It has been 20 years since they first entered my life and they are still around! I believe our spirit birds and animals bring us messages that we may or may not understand, but their presence always comforts us.

MANIFESTING LOVE

I had been single for four years! While I had no complaints about my life in general, I was alone and what is worse, I was lonely. I had scaled back work and was semi-retired due to my health and the fact that I did not really need to work. I was also coming to realize that there is just that much golf I can play. I needed companionship. I wanted a companion. Someone to share my life with. Someone to hold. Someone to love and someone who loved me.

I am quite spiritual so, I decided to ask for help from my guides and angels to help me manifest my soulmate! In my meditations, I visualized an ideal companion for me, and when I slept at night, I visualized that companion holding my hand and sleeping next to me. It was a very comforting vision and it felt oh, so real!!

A few weeks later, I was contacted for a well-paid, part time position that I really could not refuse. It checked many of the boxes for me. Short hours, good package and out of town! May be this will relieve some of the boredom and take me in a different direction. Who knows, I might even meet the companion I had been seeking!!!

I accepted the position and headed to the new city…full of hope, excitement, and anticipation…although I had no idea why a mere part-time job was bringing that on…until I walked into the office. There stood the most beautiful lady I had ever seen! Not only that, my gut told me that she was the companion I had been asking for! Later, while talking with her, I found out that she had pretty much the same reaction!

It did not take us long to discover that we loved each other and we have been blissfully and happily married since!!

ANITA'S STORIES

SPIRIT DIRECTS MY PATH

L ife even at age three was very traumatic. I really had nowhere to go and no way to escape. To cope with the fear, anxiety, and hopelessness of my situation, I would often leave my body. To this day I do not know how I learned to do that at such a young age. As I grew up, I consciously started doing that to deal with difficult situations. Someone who knew me quite well, suggested that I take some courses to better understand and work with my psychic gifts since I found myself channeling also. I became a Reiki master. I also studied mediumship.

Several years later I ran into the gentleman who had taught me to hone my abilities as a medium. It was great to see him since I had connected with his teaching methods and respected him a lot. He was now using his talents to help rescue souls that had tragic deaths, specifically murder victims. These souls seem to be stuck in limbo between the physical and the spiritual realms because of the emotional trauma attached to their deaths. I was surprised when he asked me if I would be willing to help him with some of the work. I did not know if I could, but decided to give it a try.

The soul that he was working with now, was walking, so I started walking behind her to observe what she would do. She would walk to a certain spot, where a dark entity stood by the path. She would then turn back and do the same thing again. My mentor told me to somehow persuade her to walk past that point so she could then head home instead of going around in circles endlessly. As we neared that point again, my mentor held the dark entity back, as I walked behind her and gently encouraged her to keep going forward. At this point I realized that I was no longer Anita, but a native American elder. I was able to get her to walk past the previous turning point. Lo and behold, I then saw her go up into the light. The cycle that was holding her there had been broken.

SPIRIT PROMPTS

I currently work as a relationship counsellor, so I was surprised to be called to attend a meeting with the board members of a company where a tragic event had taken place. An employee of the company had been found dead in the elevator well. The police were investigating to determine whether it was an accident, a suicide, or a murder. During this time the CEO wanted to transfer one of his staff to another location because he was a close friend of the deceased, so the CEO thought it would be less traumatic for him to be away instead of having to deal with a daily reminder. However, this gentleman kept refusing to leave without giving any reason as to why he would not do it. Since everyone had been assigned a counsellor, I wondered why they had called me in since I was a relationship counsellor. As we sat in the meeting room, and this gentleman refused to move, I was trying to figure out how I was going to approach this, when the image of an epitaph floated in my mind. Aha! It made sense! So, this is what he wanted to do. I asked him if he was insisting on staying because he wanted to create the best epitaph honoring his friend with his colleagues participating also. He was surprised and looked at me to confirm that that was the reason, although he had not known how to present it to the board so they would not think he was crazy.

The CEO was glad to discover the reason and then went to work on recruiting the deceased man's colleagues who wanted to be a part of it.

Another issue resolved with gentle prompting from my team of invisible helpers!!!!!!!!

GUIDES REDIRECT

Driving these days has become an interesting experience. I frequently find myself on roads that are unfamiliar or where I surprisingly find myself, having taken a wrong turn unconsciously and then wondering why I did it, only to find that it worked out much better than the route I was planning to take.

For example, I was on my way from London to the Lake District to attend a weekend retreat. I was running late, and realized that in my anxiety I missed the turnoff to the Motorway and had to re-route myself. I knew that it would make me even more late, so I was panicking.

I arrived at the weekend retreat, and as expected, I was late because of the unscheduled diversion, so I made my apologies! Then I looked around to see who all had already arrived only to find that none of the others were there yet. It turned out that I was not as late as everyone else because they were still stuck on the Motorway because of an accident near the exit that I inadvertently missed.

I felt blessed.

Anita Jackson is Counsellor/Psychotherapist, a Qigong Teacher. and a Reiki Master. She is also the author of Rekindle the Magic in your Relationship; Making Love Work and is passionate about helping others

Discovering the miscommunication that prevents Your Joy!
(in Work or at Home)
+44 7894 980994
www.anitajackson.co.uk
anita@anitajackson.co.uk

Danielle's Stories

Invasive Energy of a Co-worker

I was working in a small clinic in Sydney, Australia, doing Reiki and healing work. Those of us who worked there had our own cubicles, where we saw clients. The guy who worked in the next cubicle, had energy that would spill over from his room in to my room. I am very sensitive to energies around me and I found his energy to be quite controlling and always trying to connect with my energies. I was doing Reiki and healing work then. I found that I wanted to protect my space. At that time, I had not yet learnt how to control my energies and manage my space very well. So, I would fill a bucket with silver energy and throw that silver energy around my space that would make me feel protected. The next step I took was that I would put angels in the room. My angels were very military looking angels who would line both sides of the wall. That worked for a while, but even though I felt protected in my space, I could still feel his energy coming into my room.

One day I started to meditate. As I meditated, I saw a little cherub in front of me. It looked like a real angel or what we think an angel looks like based on the images we see in books or on TV. So, I asked for some more support to protect my space.

This was my first experience with angels. Until then I had not worked with any angels or did not even own a deck of angel cards. I had not felt any connection to them. I was only pulling in their energy to protect myself.

Since then, my connection has grown much stronger and now I consistently work with many of them, especially archangel Michael.

ANGELS TO THE RESCUE

These days, I have more consistent experiences with angels. After my first experience, I cautiously started to invite their help and guidance. What really opened me up to their love and help was the time when I was not in a relationship and was feeling lost. I was living by myself and had been feeling a deep sadness because of an emptiness in my life. Because I felt so empty and alone, I would ask the angels to wrap me in their wings at night so I could sleep. I started to have an amazing vision of being wrapped in a cocoon of angel wings. I found that I felt surrounded by love so I could then sleep and not feel the depth of emptiness that I normally did. I felt completely safe and supported. Now I work with angels more consistently, especially archangel Michael. I also feel the presence of many other angels who are either with me or may be around people that I work with.

I was working so many hours that I felt as if I had lost my connection to my core and did not even know why I was working so hard. When that realization hit me, I decided to reconnect with myself. To do that, I started meditating more. I was creating that space for my spiritual self in my life, while seeking answers to what was driving me. During my meditations, I heard a small voice telling me to go to New Zealand. I was not ready or willing to just pick up and move to a new place where I did not even know anyone, just to start my life over. So, I chose to ignore the voice and went about my day.

When I sat down to meditate the next day, the voice was back again, with more specific instructions. It then told me to move to New Zealand but specified that it should be the South Island.

The voice got stronger as days went by. Even though I still did not know anyone in New Zealand, I thought, well my grandfather lived on the North Island and even though he had passed now, I thought if he could do it, I could too.

Another epiphany I had was that in the classes I was teaching, I was instructing clients to walk their talk and honor their truth. I felt that I should practice what I am preaching and live my truth just as I instructed them to do. After giving it much thought, I decided to follow through. I decided that I would go for three months to test the waters. I could get a feel for the place and then decide about making the move permanent or to stay put in Australia.

I left Sydney in sweltering heat and arrived in Christchurch to freezing rain and sleet! Despite the drastic weather change, when I got off the plane, I felt the entire landscape open and say to me, "Welcome home, Danielle!' I thought to myself, but I have never been here before! Even so, it felt like I was back home!!

I spent the three months that I had allocated to the experience in Queensland in South Island. Although it is where I live now, I did not like it at the time.

After the three months it so happened that I could not leave New Zealand because my passbook was stolen and I had to stay until it was found or another solution was presented. It took another five months before it was recovered, so I spent three months in the mountains in the north end and another three months by the beach, in a town called Sumna, where I met many people from my soul family. Many crazy energies were also encountered. I swam with the dolphins, connected to the land and to the people. I had many wonderful experiences. It seemed that the loss of my passbook gave me the time and opportunity to do much more than I could have done in the three months initially planned. The unscheduled extension of my stay also gave me clarity on where I needed to redirect my energies.

Many years before this experience, I had done my training in teaching adults how to learn and grow in the holistic field. When I got back to Sydney, I started teaching massage at a college in the city, while establishing my business working on the beach. I also started to learn more holistic modalities.

One of the new modalities was about learning to heal the wounded healer. I learned the Kyron method of healing. This was originally channeled by a lady named Jan Thomas. According to her, you come into this lifetime with three wounds that you want to heal. Throughout your life you work on clearing the course of these wounds to gain a deeper understanding of yourselves and coming into your own power. I worked on that and a few other things.

After my trip to New Zealand, the push was even stronger to move there. While I was pondering on how to facilitate that, I considered taking up mountain biking quite seriously. I even signed up for a mountain bike race in New Zealand although I did not own a bike. One day at work, I was telling some colleagues about my interest in mountain biking and how I needed a bike to practice for the race. One of the gentlemen in the group said that he had three bikes in his garage. He offered to let me pick one to borrow for my practice and even take it to New Zealand for the race. I realized that once my intentions had been clearly stated, universe started magically opening. Now that the bike had been manifested, I also found a friend who would ride with me for two or more hours every day. We rode in the local area in addition to going up to the mountains to get acclimated to breathing comfortably at higher elevation and to build stamina in preparation for the mountainous terrain of New Zealand where the race was to be held.

I was now ready to go back to New Zealand for another visit and to participate in the race. I called a friend whom I had not seen in quite some time to ask if I could stay with her for two weeks. She said that she was busy and would not be able to spend time with me, but I was welcome to stay at her place. Once I got there, I found that she was not there, but I met her flat mate. He and I connected right away and enjoyed each other's company. Yes, he is my husband now!! This was in March of 2006. In April he came to visit me for three weeks and then moved to Australia in June of that year. We lived in Sydney for a year and a half. After that the earth of New Zealand was calling me once again. I had found the energy there to be more heart centered versus the physical energy of Australia. I had been doing a lot of physical work and felt the need to make a transition to doing more energy work. At the same time my husband needed to return to New Zealand to be with his two sons. We moved back in 2008 and have lived there since.

When I started doing the healing energy work with different modalities, I discovered that my clients' bodies would tell me where I needed to focus and what modality they needed for their healing.

Life continues to be magical and spiritual growth has been exponential. The connection to land, its people and my energy work is as strong as ever.

Danielle has worked in the holistic field for 20 years.

She was intuitive as a child, but she did not realize that it was part of the same thing – specially because in those days no one talked about being connected to spirit as freely as they do now.

MEETING MY HEALTH ADVISOR

Life can be a harsh teacher, but it sure teaches us some valuable lessons.

When I was in my mid 20's I was going through a phase where I felt I needed guidance from spirit as no one in my surroundings seemed to offer advice that resonated with me. I had significant health issues that needed medical attention but my family and I could not agree on the course of treatment that I wanted to follow and the one that they thought I should.

One day things had been more chaotic than usual, so I went to the beach to talk to the ocean and confide in the waves. After spending some quality time communing with nature I was driving home when suddenly I felt a presence. It felt like some spirit was accompanying me. She introduced herself as a healer, who had come in answer to my pleas for help. I was slightly apprehensive, but I was not afraid.

When I got home, I still felt the spirit with me and when I asked her name, she said "Sophia, with a P-H." I giggled to myself.

Mom was not yet home. Sophia then proceeded to direct me to prepare dinner for both of us, something that I rarely did. Her instructions were not only voiced in my mind, but I felt them in my chest area which seemed to be pulled into whatever direction was next. Instructions were given in detail, from how low to set the flame to how much butter to add, to how and what seasonings to use…even how long to cook the filet of fish on each side. I do not recall what side dishes were prepared. I went and laid out the table and set the food since I knew my mom would be home at any moment.

I laughed as Sophia told me to heat up a bowl of dal (lentils) also for Mom as the fish dinner would not be enough for her.

I do not know what seasonings I used, how I cooked it or what recipe I followed, but dinner was delicious! Sophia felt that as we ate dinner, we could amicably discuss my treatment options after telling mom about the experience of my meeting with her.

Just as I was done setting it all up, the door opened and mom came in. We greeted each other. I asked her to set her things down so she could come and join me at the table. She did as she was asked, came to the table, and sat there looking at me with a million questions in her eyes! As she glanced at the dining table, she wondered what was going on, because as I mentioned earlier, I never cooked! I guided her to do just as Sophia had instructed me to do. I asked her to just listen without asking questions while I explained what had happened. This was simply something spirit had told me to do for her. We both enjoyed the delicious meal with a new understanding, although it was still a long time before the health issues were fully addressed.

Note: Just because guidance is received, it does not mean the problems go away magically. You need to understand and interpret the messages correctly and then actually make decisions and take actions before any resolution can be reached. There were still egos to be dealt with and disagreements to be agreed upon!

FINDING SOPHIA

A few days after my meeting with Sophia, I got a call asking if I could dog-sit. I had an on-call dog sitting gig for a beautiful pup named Kaya, usually overnight and occasionally a weekend. I was paid generously for something I loved to do anyway. I got to spend a nice relaxing weekend with Kaya and got paid for it! What could be better? When the client returned from her trip and proceeded to pay me the $150 that she owed, she found that she did not have change and neither did I. In her generosity, she just told me to keep the change from the two $100 bills. It certainly made my day!

On a side note, Mom and I would often go to the library and buy used books. Over the years we had picked up many interesting and some out-of-print books too, so we looked forward to it. When these were on sale, it was even better! On one such visit to a local library, we had picked up two copies of a book called 'The Secret of the Butterfly Lovers: Eternal Lessons of Life, Love and Reincarnation' by Keith Richardson. One of the copies was even autographed! We both read through our copies and compared notes and discussed content as if we were part of a book club. We also discovered that the author had an angel store not too far away. We talked about going to visit it one day because we would need to plan the trip since it was far enough to take at least half a day for the trip.

Well, that one day came sooner than we had thought. One of my best friends was having a birthday party for her child and she lived just a few miles past the Angel store. We would be driving right by it! We decided that we would stop there on our way back from the party.

Now, I love spiritual shops but this one felt magical even in the entryway. This was my signal from Spirit that something cool was about to take place.

The store was empty except for the two people behind the counter, who were none other than the author Keith Richardson and his wife – the owners of the store and the people we were hoping to meet!! We were so excited to meet this lovely and loving couple. They were very friendly and just as excited to talk about their book with someone who had read it and could relate. They shared some interesting stories about their experiences and some insights about the writing of the book. During our intriguing conversation, they described what their shop was about and how they supported local artists. They had an area at the back of the store where people could write their wishes onto a sticky paper and place it on the wall. They had many types of art displayed on their wall which included handmade wooden angels that stood about a foot high. While they told us a little bit about all the artists, they specially talked about one artist who had had a near death experience (NDE). When he came out of a coma, and was well enough to get back to work, he found that he was able to make wooden angels, in a very special way, considering he had no experience doing any kind of wood work before. He now used thinly 'sliced' pieces of wood to create his artwork. This story fascinated me, so I started looking at his work that the owners had hanging on the wall.

And then I saw her in her beautiful green and amber tones. I immediately felt a connection and a pull. I felt as if I knew her. I asked for the price and was told that it was two-hundred dollars – the exact amount I had with me from the dog sitting! I would normally have deposited the money since I do not like to carry too much cash, but I had not had a chance to go the bank yet! Now I knew why!! As if that was not magical enough, when Keith was taking her down from the wall, he mentioned that the artist likes to name the angels he makes. I turned it around to look for her name on the back, and there it was – "Sophia," with a PH. It was one of those pieces that he had dropped off just the day before.

After I picked up 'my Sophia,' we walked out of the back room to pay for it. As we did, the store started to fill up and it was so full by the time we walked out that there was no room left for any more people to walk in. Keith told us that this is how busy the store usually is. He was surprised that when we got there, there was no one else in the store for almost a half hour.

With tears streaming down my face from joy, excitement, relief- and numerous other feelings, in my heart and my mind I expressed gratitude for the entire experience.

LISA'S STORIES

WELCOME NEW NEIGHBOR!

I am an intuitive psychic medium and I communicate with my guides daily. I have many stories but here is a fun one!

Two years ago, my husband and I moved to a new community where we did not know anyone. A week after we had arrived, I went to shop for essentials. While walking into the store I had a conversation with my spiritual guides, saying that I need to find a friend as I would be lonely otherwise. After about ten minutes, as I walked around the aisle, this lady came by pushing her trolley. As she walked past me, she said,

"I love the color of your top!" I thanked her and walked on. As soon as she said that, my guides told me that I need to go and talk to her. I asked them what they wanted me to do. Stalk her?

A loud 'YES!' was the response from my guides! They said just imagine if she lived on your street?

So, I started thinking of an excuse to chat with her as I was trying to find her again in Countdown. When I caught up to her, I asked her where a certain product was in this store as I was new to the area. The lady then asked me where I lived. I told her the street name and she said that she lived on the same street. What number? She asked. When I said we were in number 38, she told me she lived in number 19.

An excited conversation followed, during which she mentioned that she is a Reiki Master! That was the icing on the cake for me!

Since then, we have become great friends and our husbands bonded as well.

I am very humbled and grateful that my guides picked out just the right friend for me.

Guardian Angel

When I turned nineteen years old, I decided to go with a few friends on the big OE (Overseas Experience) and then work in England as a nanny. I had been on a Contiki bus tour for six weeks throughout Europe when I got the Contiki cough virus. As the tour ended my friends and I went our separate ways. Sadly, I ended up back in London in a shabby bedsit, sick, homesick, and wondering what I should do next.

I am glad I listened to my gut feeling and instead of staying to work as a nanny, I bought a one-way direct flight ticket to get back home to New Zealand. In addition to being really scared to travel alone, I was coughing almost non-stop, to the point where I felt like I was going to be sick. I got to Heathrow airport only to find that thick fog had closed the airport.

While sitting and waiting for the fog to clear, I heard a woman, not far from me, talking to someone. She sounded like a Kiwi! I was excited to hear a familiar accent. I saw her walk over towards me and sit in a chair right next to me. I struck up a conversation with her in the hope that she too may be heading back to New Zealand. We introduced ourselves. When I told her my name, with great delight she told me she had flown over to see her daughter whose name is also Lisa. It so happened that her daughter was working as a nanny in Paris, which is what I was hoping to do too, but in London. Her daughter was having problems, so she had come to spend some time with her. She then asked me my middle name, which is Jane, which coincidentally also happened to be her daughter's middle name.

Miraculous synchronicity continued as she told me that she lived in Auckland, and yes you guessed it! It is where I also lived! As I dug deeper and asked where in Auckland she lived, her reply was Howick. By this time, I was thinking, "Wow! Someone is definitely watching out for me," since I am from Howick too. Then to burst all expectations she was on the same flight, merely two rows in front of me!

Surely, she was the angel sent to look out for me that day. She helped me on and off the plane. I felt safe and comforted, knowing I was not alone and was being taken care of.

HEALING NEEDED

When I was growing up, my mum's best friend lived just across the road from us. I looked upon her as my second mum, which is why Lois has always been very special to me.

Early one morning I was awakened by a male voice talking to me. He asked me to please send healing to Lois.

Suddenly wide awake and wondering what was going on with Lois, I sat with my spiritual team and sent healing to her. Afterwards I called mum on the phone and told her about my conversation with this man. Apparently, Lois had gone to England to visit family four weeks earlier. We knew she was due home sometime that week but we were not sure on details.

We then found out that when I received the message to send healing to her, she was aboard a plane on her way home to New Zealand. As soon as she arrived, she was rushed to the hospital because her whole body was swollen and she had been in heart failure.

I felt very privileged to be contacted to help her. Another timely message of healing from the other side!

MORE HEALING AND COMFORTING...

Just a couple of weeks ago I ended up taking my dad to the hospital as he had fluid in the lungs. I always ask my spiritual team to get us into the hospital ward with ease and grace since our hospital is always overflowing with patients and usually there are no beds free. So sure enough, in answer to my prayers, dad went straight into the adult assessment wing. Everything was moving in the flow as I had requested.

Just then I received a text to say that my second mum Lois was in the hospital because they suspected she had a small stroke.

Straight away my intuition sparked and I felt a synchronicity taking place. When I texted back to ask where in the hospital she was, I was told that she was in the same wing as my dad. So, I asked the nurse if they have Lois in the ward and sure enough, she was merely three rooms away!

As her daughter could not reach her till the next day, it was divine timing that I could be there with her until then.

A WARNING

M y dad was in his late seventies and very fit for his age. Most days he would walk a track through native bush that had over forty stairs. On this day when I had popped in to say hi, he was dressed in his shorts, ready to go on this track walk.

As he walked past me, he put his hand on my shoulder and said I am going now. No sooner had he put his hand on my shoulder that I got a feeling as if I had been punched in my solar plexus (Chakra below the navel) I intuitively felt like he was saying goodbye to me...as if he could die.

I was shocked with what I felt but I held back my emotions and said goodbye. I got in my car to head home, still stunned by this feeling. I turned on the car and the radio came alive and the song that was playing was 'I'm going to miss you when you are gone.'

With tears streaming I knew that this was a sign that something was going to take place for my dad. I just did not know when. I rang my sister-in-law to give her the heads up of what I felt.

Her response was a firm denial because she thought he was too healthy for anything like that. Well, within a month my dad became very sick and we nearly lost him. He was diagnosed with Lymphoma, a type of blood cancer. Fortunately, it is a smoldering type of cancer so it grows over a long period of time before a person dies. As I write this my dad has turned ninety years old. He has only twenty percent of his heart muscle working and has the lymphoma. He still takes care of my mum at home. We are very blessed to still have him.

GUT FEELING SAVES MY LIFE

I had been going to a specialist for the past eight years. Each year I would have a mammogram and ultrasound on my breasts. My mother had breast cancer and I had twenty fibroid lumps in both breasts. Hence the need to keep an eye on them yearly.

On the ninth year just before my visit to the specialist I became very agitated and felt I wanted both breasts to be removed. I felt like I was carrying a bomb on my chest. Friends told me not to be silly. They said that I will be fine since the annual exams were not indicating any adverse results. And yet this nagging feeling refused to go away.

So, when I went to my appointment, I told the specialist that I wanted both my breasts removed. He told me that you have just done your mammogram and ultrasound, and everything looks ok. He also mentioned that because the tests showed no cancer, the insurance will not pay for it.

When I still insisted on having both my breasts removed, to appease me he ordered an MRI. A week later, I had the MRI. The specialist rang up to tell me that the scan was all good and no cancer was found. However, a week later he rang again and in a very serious voice told me that a second doctor had looked at my results and they had found two potentially cancerous lumps.

I had a biopsy done on them.

When I got home, in the lounge I saw a shredded monarch butterfly that the cat had brought in. Butterflies are one of my signs, so I knew that the results would come back positive for cancer.

I firmly believe in divine timing for everything. Earlier in the year, my husband had decided that I should get life insurance since he also had it. The policy had a three- month probation period. If I had been diagnosed on the first phone call after the MRI, I would not have been able to collect on my claim. The second call received a week later, putting it past the probationary period allowed me to get the $50,000 payout for a life-threatening illness per the clause we had in the insurance policy. My husband and I did not need to stress financially when he took time off work to look after me. I was and am so blessed.

Blessings did not end there!

Surgery to remove both my breasts and reconstruct them was going to take approximately twelve hours. I wanted my husband to be there when I came out of surgery and knew twelve hours was going to make it a very late night for him. I asked the surgeon if she had ever done a surgery in nine hours. She said everything would have to work perfectly, with no glitches and even then, she was not sure if she could do it in nine hours.

Being a hypnotherapist, I know the power of the mind. I spoke to my body and explained what was going to happen and that I needed everything to go right so the surgeon could complete the surgery in around nine hours.

When I came to after the big day, my first question to the surgeon was how long did the surgery take? Lo and behold, it was nine hours and fifteen minutes.

My life is full of synchronicity and because I am aware and expect it to work that way, I do not place any negativity or blocks in its path. I also accept that when it does not work as I ask for it, it is either because something better is to come in a different way or I may have misinterpreted a message. In all this though, I never question the divine help and guidance!

Spirits Support

In this story I wanted to share how spirit supported me on this journey through the peaks and valleys as my dad moved closer to the date of his passing.

My dad reached his 90th birthday which was a wonderful family celebration. Relatives flew in or traveled up in their camper vans from out of town to be part of dad's birthday because he was the last Uncle left alive.

Not long after that I felt he was on the decline and felt he was starting his transitioning journey. He had just got out of hospital after three days and seemed fine when suddenly three hours later his vitals dropped and he was rushed back to the hospital.

He became unconscious and my two brothers and I took turns to be at his side, so he was not alone. I took the afternoon and night shifts. On the second night I sent a prayer asking if my dad could be taken as he was suffering. I heard a loud voice in my head from my guide and it sounded like I was being chided like a child. I was told "He has his own agenda, and you are the by-stander."

I took this to mean that dad had his own timing and I needed to be patient and allow things to be. So, I knew divine timing was playing a part in dad's journey. On the third night as I sat next to dad in the early hours of the morning, I felt a pressure on my cheek as if someone had kissed me and wondered if it was dad saying goodbye.

On the fourth day before my shift which was sixteen hours long, I felt a rising of anxiety in my body and was feeling overwhelmed about the situation. My mum who also struggles with her own conditions had spent one night up at the hospital on the first night that dad was in and unfortunately caught influenza A. This was another worry. So, I decided to sit and meditate.

Note from Lisa: I share the following details of my communication with spirit and the responses and messages I received about my dad's transition, in the hope that these may be helpful to those who might be wondering if their loved one might be suffering in their last moments or struggling to understand and accept their final transition.

I asked my team about dad's condition and what was happening with him as he progressed closer to death. I heard them say that the night I had felt the kiss was my dad saying goodbye to me. In my dad's case his main expression of frequency had departed but a filament thread of frequency was left behind as the body was starting to decommission. Like a computer defragging the programs or in his case his internal body functions breaking down.

After hearing this information, I felt like a ton of bricks had been lifted from my shoulders and I could see my dad in a different light and knew that he was not suffering.

On the fifth day as I was sitting with mum at her house talking about dad, I told her that I have a feeling that a spiritual being is standing beside me no matter where I go. Then it suddenly dawned on me that I had asked my team to give me a heads up when dad was close to passing. I asked them to stand close as an indicator.

My middle brother was sitting with dad at the time of my realization of dad's indication of passing and I still had some hours before my turn. My brother had never liked hospitals let alone sitting with the sick and it was his greatest fear that dad would go on his watch. What you fear you could attract, and my older brother and I both said it will be on his watch.

So, knowing spirit had given me the sign that dad was passing that day I went to the hospital before my shift was to start. As I got to the door a nurse walked out and I saw my brother in tears saying dad had just passed. It was beautiful that we could both be together at that time to support each other which I am sure dad planned that way.

A day later as I sat with family members talking about dad, I got a message from him loud and clear "*You could have burnt me in my crocks*" (favorite shoes).

Mum had sent up the slippers she disliked for dad to be cremated in. Dad loved his crocks and would wear them every day if he was allowed to because mum thought they looked scruffy. The family got such a lift knowing dad still had one over mum even in death. So, he got his crock shoes before he was cremated the following day.

A few days later Mum also went downhill with influenza A and a bacterial infection. I took her to see the doctor who said she needed to be taken into hospital as her vitals were not doing so well. She was scared and fearful of going into hospital as we had just lost dad only days ago.

She thought she would not make it out alive. I felt her life hung in the balance. Mum was moved around in the hospital to three different wards and ended up in the same ward as the one that dad had passed in.

I had felt quite numb after dad had gone and then the uncertainty of mum hung heavy over me. When I found out which ward she was in and before getting out of my car to visit, this huge emotion seemed to erupt, and I had to sit in the car for a little bit to compose myself before visiting her. When I got to her ward, I saw that her bed was right across the hall from where dad had passed. I knew this had to be orchestrated by spirit in some way as I do not believe in coincidences. I asked spirit why this had happened, and I was told that it was for my wellbeing as we needed to release. Mum did come home to recover three days later.

I had tickets to a dance production that both of my granddaughters were dancing in. As I was watching the show my attention got pulled to the aisle steps and as I looked, I saw a man's leg pop out on the stairs for a short stretch wearing the same color crocks that dad wore.

I intuitively knew dad was saying thanks, I got the crocks.

As I reflect on my dad's journey, I recall that he had fractured his lower back and got the results just days before he went into hospital for the last time. It showed that there was the start of bone cancer. What he died from was blood poisoning. I believe that it was his best option to depart on his terms rather than go through a long and painful blood cancer option of departure.

I feel humbled by the support that my spiritual team showed me during dad's journey and am grateful for dad reaching out to tell me to get his crocks. I still hear from him from time to time.

Note: Three months after my dad's passing, mom decided to join him and gave up her struggle. While I miss them both I am sure they are happy to resume their journey together after sixty-two years together on earth.

Lisa Thomas is a psychic intuitive, medium, empath, Channeler & hypnotherapist. She helps to shift people's focus to enable them to reconnect with their inner wisdom and grow from life's experiences so they can align with who they want to become.

lisa@tgl.co.nz Website: lisathomasintuitive.com

Raj's Story

Life works in mysterious ways and in hindsight we can see the guiding hand of our invisible helpers at work in directing the course of our lives to where our hearts desire to go, even though sometimes the path is a bit convoluted. This is how my destiny directed me to be where I needed to be, to get what I really wanted.

I was working on my college degree and since I absolutely love international travel, it had been my dream for a long time to do a study semester abroad. It was a dream that was not being realized because whenever it was time to fill out paperwork, I would talk myself out of the final step of obtaining letters of recommendation for it. I felt that I just did not have the independence and confidence to be out in the world away from all that I knew and what I was comfortable with. Besides, it sounded like a chore I did not want to take time for, so I lost interest at that point of the process.

When I joined Cal State University, Long Beach, I started taking focused foreign language college courses and advanced courses, I felt somewhat more confident and ready to venture forth. I went to see the head of the languages department to seek advice on it. I was told that they felt I would do better as an exchange student in Switzerland. It would not just be a semester abroad with other students and American peers but essentially what is a language immersion where I would exchange places with a student in their school. How many times had I talked myself out of going because I did not feel ready to do this on my own? Hence, I was surprised to find that I was onboard with this program even though it was scarier! It would even be in a country that I had not considered as an option even though it is beautiful and was on my bucket list of places to visit.

In spring of 2003, I felt brave and ready to venture out in to unknown territory. I felt I was somehow "spiritually encouraged." I finally had everything ready to go. Signed, sealed, and *almost* delivered. I had the envelope ready to go for days or maybe even weeks – I do not quite recall now, but it was longer than it needed to be. One day I pushed myself to go and drop it in the mailbox as I gave myself a pep talk – *Come on! You have made it this far, now go!* I pictured myself with envelope in hand, standing in front of the blue mailbox, with my hand on the handle, pulling the slot open ready to drop it in…. but I just could not do it. Something was certainly holding me back. I did not question it, but just left and never looked back.

In October 2003, I decided I wanted to get married. Since I was not dating anyone and had not really met anyone that I was interested in marrying, I figured I would check out the Indian matrimonial website. There, I met a guy with whom I felt a connection. Everything lined up quickly and we got married. I also realized that if I had gone to Switzerland, this would not have happened. I completed my Bachelor's degree and in November 2004, I moved to St Louis vicinity where my husband lived. He was in real estate and was established in his business, so he did not wish to move to California. I too felt that it would be beneficial for me as I started a new phase of my life as a married lady. Unfortunately, even though we remained friends, our marriage did not work out to be the happily ever after type. Although legally we were married for seven and a half years for about four of those years I wanted out. He was a very nice guy but there were major differences in what each one of us wanted out of this marriage. The biggest hurdle that neither of us was willing to compromise on was that I wanted a family and he did not. My friends were surprised that we had not discussed such an important aspect. Well, in our culture, no discussion is needed when a man is ready to 'settle down,' because it is a given that he is ready to take on the responsibility of a family. I just felt stuck in life and needed to move on. At this point, I wanted to come back home to California, so I used my mom's address on my resumes and applied for jobs but got no responses at all.

For the most part the period between Christmas and New Year, we would go to California to celebrate time off and my birthday. But in 2009 I had been unemployed, so financially it was a strain and I could not afford to do so. My husband and I had talked about separation and divorce, but were allowing time to process it before making a final decision. My husband went to India to visit family, but I stayed back since I was still applying for jobs and hoping to hear back from some of the companies. To make matters worse, I got very sick. Several days and nights of 103 degree fever and deep cough that would not quit left me feeling a little depressed and feeling sorry for myself.

On 12/31/09, I was still feeling a little sick, so I was lying in bed, when a friend called to ask if I wanted to join her and some others for a New Year's Eve party. At first, I said no because the venue was a forty-minute drive from my home and all I wanted to do was sleep. Then I thought – well in addition to being New Year's Eve, it would also be a birthday celebration for me, so why not make the effort? I figured I would get up and get dressed, then see how I felt. It would be fun to see my friends and enjoy the change of scene, since I was still legally married, even though we were talking about divorce by then. I got to the venue by 10pm and stood in line for a while. I looked around to spot my friend, walked fast to cut through the crowd and found her at this long table where she and her friends were sitting.

I also observed that some guys were standing behind the table. I made eye contact with one of them. For a while we kept eyeing each other from our tables, but did not look at each other while I danced with my friends. This continued for quite a while. My friends also thought that these guys were cute. By now, we were trying to figure out how to talk to them. One of them looked like a very young twenty-five-year-old college kid so I decided to just have some fun making eye-contact and smiling at him, since technically I was still married.

A little later, I decided to break the ice. I bought him and his friends a round of shots and said to them, "You guys are just standing there not having fun-so here you go!"

Now that certainly broke the ice and after that we spent the rest of the evening dancing. Well, it turned out that he was not a twenty-five-year-old college kid, but a thirty-eight-year-old school teacher. Unfortunately, with all that dancing and icy drinks, my cough kicked up and got the best of me. As much as I wanted this fun evening to continue, I opted to head home since it was past midnight after exchanging phone numbers. I called him the next morning to see if he wanted to meet for coffee. And as they say…. The rest became our future!

Note: We are now blessed with three beautiful children and the family I always envisioned. Unfortunately, my ex-husband died of a heart attack a few years later. I realized that had I not redirected my life where Spirit guided me to, I would not have had the family I wanted, but I would have lost him anyway.

A round 1981 when I was about twenty-one or so I left Canada and moved to Florida. There, I started speaking to my spirit guides more frequently to ask for help in resolving some issues in my life. With their help and guidance, I became more aware of the presence of my team of helpers and got in touch with my spiritual self. A deep spiritual experience in 1987 brought a major shift in my life. It transformed how I viewed others around me. It taught me to judge less and see beauty in everything. I also began to be more receptive to the messages I was receiving from my guides, which I had been ignoring before.

One day as I was sitting under a palm tree – I felt what I perceived as the voice of God reverberate through me. It stated – You will move to Australia. Now, how did I know that it was the voice of God? I simply felt it. Of course, me being who I was – someone who knew what was best for me and who made my own decisions, I said 'no' because I had only one year left before I qualified for my green card, and I did not plan to give that up for anything!!

Well, one thing led to another and within the year, I had moved to Australia. I packed and shipped eleven boxes of my things to Australia. I sold everything else. During that time, I had a dream.!! In my dream, I had seen Australia with its red brick buildings like tenement buildings of New York rather than the icing sugar pastel colors of Florida that I had imagined it to be. I figured it was only a dream, so I was not too concerned. However, when I finally reached Australia, I noticed that the buildings were just as I had seen them in my dream, which felt more like a nightmare now. I felt a pang of regret merely after my first busy day and I questioned my decision to move wondering if I had been impulsive. So, instead of making another impulsive decision, I decided to stay and see how it would play out.

In due course, I met and married a man who was a bricklayer. I felt that somehow that was not right since in Florida I had a vision, where I saw myself living on a cattle property. This ranch was set back far enough from the main road to where the house was not immediately visible. Where I now lived with my husband was nothing like that. It turned out that this was another impulsive decision that had to be reversed. Things turned sour quickly with my bricklayer husband and we filed for divorce.

After that, I moved on with my life and focused on my work. Even though I was lonely, I decided to take a break from dating to get my life back on course.

Not long after, on a Country Golf Day, I met someone who is a grazier, which is an Australian version of a cowboy. Although we both felt the sparks fly, I distinctly heard a voice in my head warning me that 'he would hurt me badly.' I heeded that voice and did not let myself be drawn into a relationship for two years. Even though I resisted for quite a long time, he was persistent and eventually I broke down. We started dating. We got married and settled into a life of homesteaders. This home was just as I had seen in my vision, built in the middle of nowhere and it was set back far enough from the road and was not visible from there.

Once again, just as I had received the warning, which I disregarded, it did not take very long for him to hurt me. We divorced and yet again I had set myself back.

Our guides advise us and guide us, but since we have free will, we must ask for help. The lesson I learned from this was that when we ask and manifest things in our life, we need to be very specific and literal! Having received that advice and guidance, we also need to heed it and not ignore it, since it is coming from a higher perspective and is not ego-based. I have often wondered if I experienced the hurt because it was pre-ordained for me to learn certain lessons or was it because I chose to go that way even though I had been warned. Either way, our choices determine the course of our life and even the bad ones have value only if we learn from them.

Now, here I was, a single mother in dire straits once again. I felt lost and very alone. In despair, I asked the guides what I should do for work that would give me financial security while allowing time to raise my child. The word 'life coach' popped in my head. This line of work was new and not too many people in Australia had heard about it. However, I was able to find a niche market where there was great need for it. Spirit led me to a documentary about the social and emotional needs of children who are victims of domestic violence and/or abuse. As victims, frequently women have their needs addressed and they receive the help needed. However, the children, whose life is also turbulent and is being shaped by these traumatic events, are further traumatized by being shuttled from place to place and from other child care services without their individual needs being addressed. Divine guidance helped me to discover this award- winning program and I was able to make a difference for thousands of children and families as well as supporting myself and my young son for fifteen years. Again, spirit has guided me to help others with new modalities.

Sissy Mylrea lives in Australia and has worked with many different modalities in the spiritual field. She is a trained Counsellor, NLP Life Coach, Introspective Hypnosis Therapist and does Biofield Tuning. She is constantly learning to listen to spirit and trust the process, so she does not push back too much. With practice the process is becoming smoother and information is flowing more easily as she moves out of her own way not expecting it to come a certain way, but by simply allowing it to proceed naturally.

Sissy can be reached at mmylrea1@bigpond.com

My Stories

MY TEAM PUSHES ME TOWARDS MY PURPOSE

I had a follow up appointment after my cataract surgery. My eye was still healing and it had to be dilated, which meant that my vision would not be normal for a few hours, so I had to arrange for a ride. I mostly preferred afternoon appointments because California traffic is brutal in the mornings and evenings aka the rush hours! The doctor's office was a good one hour plus drive from home. As always, my daughter came to my rescue.

One day before my appointment, the doctor's office called to say that the doctor had to perform an emergency surgery in the afternoon, so would I be able to get there by 7:00 AM or would I prefer to reschedule. Time change was the lesser of two evils since we had both taken a sick day from work.

One of my friends lived very close to the doctor's office, whom I had not seen in a long time because of the distance and our schedules. My daughter asked if we could visit her since we will be driving by her house anyway. We called her and it worked out great! She was home, and the visit would allow us to miss the rush hour instead of sitting on the freeway for hours. We spent the morning catching up, enjoying a cup of tea and a lovely breakfast. My daughter, played with her dog and chatted with her, while I lay with my eyes closed to rest and relax.

When we got home, we had lunch and enjoyed a restful siesta. As we woke up and headed to the kitchen for a cup of tea, my daughter asked if we could attend a book signing at a new age book store that my friend had told her about. We had no plans for the evening, so I thought, why not?

The author was Gary Quinn, and the book was a self-help book. The event was well attended. This was his third book, but I had not heard of him before. My friend was there as well. I purchased my copy and got in line for Gary to sign it.

That evening, I started to read his book 'The Yes Frequency,' and I could not put it down. As I sat at my desk, reading late into the night, I came to a part where he mentioned that he also offered certification for life coaching. This had been my wish and ardent desire – to be a life coach! I emailed him right away. I signed up for the course and have been on that path.

With a gentle nudge from my team on the other side, that meeting and the content of the book guided me towards the general direction of my purpose and it helped me to start the journey that I had been procrastinating for a long time.

I SEEK HELP AND RECEIVE IT IN A MOST DRAMATIC WAY!

*Even though the story of this meeting is shared in my first book,
'How to Help Yourself to Be Who You Want to Be' I feel it bears repeating in this book too.*

I had been having health issues that were not responding to medication. It was now at the point where the surgery my doctor had suggested was not an option anymore; it was necessary.

My husband and I discussed our finances, because even with insurance, the co-pay for the doctor fees and hospital bills would be sizeable. We had taken some hits with our business, and a one-week stay in the hospital following surgery would not be cheap, so it was a major concern.

To prepare for that, we called the insurance company and were assured that all was good. They would pay 80 percent of both the doctor's fee and the hospital bill, and we would have to pay 20 percent per the terms of our policy.

After the surgery when I came home, we called to follow up with the insurance company about how and where to submit the bills. We were shocked to find out that the insurance company had gone under and would no longer pay any of the bills. Overnight, we were liable for the entire 100 percent of all the bills.

We were certainly not prepared for this expense, but it was what it was. We called the hospital to explain the situation and negotiate monthly payments after making a down payment. The gentleman we spoke with was very helpful, and we settled on the amount we would need to pay per month until the balance was paid in full. The 20 percent we had budgeted was used to pay the doctor's fee in full, so that helped.

After we had sent in our second payment to the hospital, we got a call from one of their representatives, demanding payment in full. When I explained about the negotiated payments, he said that the person we had made the arrangement with was not authorized to do so and, if we did not pay the full balance within the week, they would take us to court. With everything that was going on, in addition to my painful recovery, I was overwhelmed. That night, when I could not sleep, I got down on my knees, and with tears streaming down my face, I asked God why all this was happening. After all, we were working hard to earn an honest living and trying to do the right thing but were falling deeper and deeper into the hole. I pleaded for help.

After that I lay down in bed again, I must have fallen asleep, because I recall being woken up by a presence in my room. With my eyes half open, I felt that this presence was greater than me and that I could not receive it lying down. I had to sit up out of respect. When I opened my eyes, I saw a huge, pale-gold ball of shimmering light from floor to ceiling. It felt very comforting. I just knew that things would be okay. I did not ask how, when, why, or where, but I knew I did not need to worry about it any longer. I lay down again and slept like a baby, wrapped in its warmth.

When I woke up the next day, I felt very lighthearted.

About a week after my experience, I was at work in our retail store, helping a customer, when the new salesgirl came to ask me the price of a dress that another customer was inquiring about. The dress was from a recently arrived shipment that I had not tagged yet. I asked her to help my customer, and I went to help the other lady.

As I approached her, she put back the dress she was holding, pointed to me and said, "You! You're the one. You have been asking the Spirits for help. They have sent me to help you!'

It had been a week since my experience, I was now at work and in a different mindset, so while a part of my brain listened to her, in the other part, I questioned myself, wondering what she was talking about. While she was telling me things about me that no one else would know, to validate what she was saying, a part of me was going along with what she was telling me. She assured me that everything would work out.

A few days later, I learned that a family friend who is an attorney was going to help us handle the case at a greatly discounted rate.

The hospital filed a case against us, but on the day of the court date, no one from the hospital showed up, so our attorney was able to negotiate a greatly reduced settlement!

Moral

There are forces in the universe that surround us and are always ready to help, if only we know and ask for their help. Knowing that we attract to us what we are, we must learn to encourage only positive thoughts and let only positive people surround us.

MY VAN AND THE ANGEL 'COP'

We had sold our business, and I was working for a very inconsiderate boss. I needed that job, so I plodded along, waiting, and praying for something better to open. One day, there was a very bad storm, where some small cars had been blown off the road. That morning, I left for work much earlier to allow extra time for the commute. Weather was not good and traffic was bad. Even so, I arrived four minutes after 8:00 AM, which was my start time. My boss was standing at the door. He looked at his watch, looked at me and told me that I was four minutes late!!!

A few weeks after that, when I was heading to work, my van sputtered just as I was getting on the freeway. I panicked and sent out a plea to my team! I said, 'You know I need this job to put food on the table. You know I need the van to get to work. You do know I do not have the money for repairs. Please help and do not let this van break down!'

I felt calm. I had elevated my problem to a Higher Power and now it was not for me to worry about it being resolved. That day I reached work on time with no more mishaps.

In the evening when I was heading home, I saw a police car parked on the side of the freeway. I glanced over and wondered what or who he was waiting for. A little while later, I saw him merge into traffic and move into a lane to my right. Was he trying to pull me over? Had I missed something? But he was looking at me and smiling, not asking me to pull over. I smiled back and thought to myself…. Okay, what is going on here? I kept glancing over while watching where I was going and he was there for several minutes. But when I glanced over once again, there was no police car…anywhere on the freeway and traffic was tight, so where and how he disappeared that fast, I really do not know.

I thought about that and wondered what that was all about. It was very odd!

When I got home, I shared that incident with my daughters. They said that maybe it was an angel trying to let me know that all would be well.

In hindsight, I believe that that was exactly what it was. After that the van rarely broke down – maybe twice, and that too when I had the money for repairs and never at a place where I would have been stranded.

As I clear the debris from my soul, the path gets clearer.

I was struggling with laziness and other soul issues that I was not clear on, but knew that they were dragging me down. I had started to work on my book, but did not always feel motivated even though when I did push myself, I felt better and more energetic. Some days I just did not feel like doing anything and I felt that I was wasting my time. It is true that I was still recovering from surgery and my body was healing slowly when some dental issues surfaced, setting me back once more. I prayed and asked my guides to help me clear my heart, mind, and soul of whatever was holding me back and delaying my stepping up to fulfill my purpose.

A few days before that, I had seen a workshop posted that was to be in Hawaii, conducted by Alba Weinman, Jill Cole and Blair Styra, three people I had been following for some time and I was very excited for the opportunity to meet them in a small class setting. Details for booking were to be posted soon. I was checking for that posting diligently since their workshops sell out fast!

Lo and behold, two days later I saw a post that registration was open to sign up for the event with Alba Weinman in which she mentioned that only two spots were left. Well, I knew her events sold out fast so I quickly pulled out my credit card to register and process the payment. I was very happy when I got the confirmation email…but wait a minute! This is not the event I thought I was signing up for! It was with the same teacher but a different event, different venue, and different dates!!! I thought of cancelling but then decided that there must be a reason that my guides had led me to this event. When I read the title and the description again, I realized, it was a very specific answer to my request to my guides for help that I had sent out two days ago.

I realized that if I went to this event, I would not be able to go to the other one that I had originally wanted to sign up for. Somehow, the excitement that I had felt about the Hawaii event before had cooled down and I felt very detached from it. At the Maryland event that I signed up for, I found out that the Hawaii event had been cancelled altogether due to some unavoidable issues!!

BLAIR STYRA

B lair Styra is a psychic medium, channel, and author. His journey to his current spiritual path, along with some deep insights about spirituality are both documented in his books 'Don't Change the Channel' and 'Who Catharted.' He can be reached for personal readings via his website www.tabaash.com.

The following excerpt is shared from his book 'Who Catharted.', Ozark Mountains Publishing, with permission from the author.

New Earth Energy and what it means.......
Being GOD more!

In the New Year…

You have 12 new chapters

You have 365 new chances

Waiting for you.

(…) This is obviously a significant time in Earth's history as it sheds some old layers and empties itself of energy that is no longer considered necessary. We are used to the belief, that when we look at something, you believe that what you see is true and absolute and constant in its finite existence. Of course, all life is infinite in its evolution and you must create a new platform for the new energy to thrive. If you as people can understand this, then you can be in harmony with these changes and subsequently make your own personal changes to align with the new energy. In fact, you *MUST* make the changes if you are to continue your time here on Earth. And this is when as true believers of the New Earth Energy you look toward advancing yourselves in the ways you can make possible. This is very exciting. You have 365 days to prepare, create and participate in a whole new way of being that engages us in positive evolution.

So, where do you start? I've compiled a list of what I believe are changes you can make that align with the New Earth Energy.

- *BE GOD CONSCIOUSLY*

From the moment you awaken, affirm in your own way and words that you indeed are *GOD*. And what greater starting point can you have to begin a day considering this is the point of creation, a point where all the power is? Whatever you need for the day, it's going to start from this place.

- *CREATE THE DAY AND ALL IT ENTAILS FOR YOU*

The day is before you and you have all the infinite possibilities of what it could be. Whatever the structure of your day, inform your life from your *GOD NATURE* the rules of the day and the outcomes that you choose to create. Information you pass on to your human nature daily is essential to a greater outcome.

- *NURTURE*

It's your day, your creation, relax and start this new day with peace and ease, knowing that all the systems that make you, are going to work better when you have a relaxed beginning. Don't rush your breakfast; use it as a time to awaken to the day, it's a good preparation time.

- *MEDITATE*

Create some time to go within and visit your higher nature and the places that exist deep within you. Allow yourself to know that through this you are *SOURCE ENERGY* and connecting in this way will enhance the day that you have before you.

- *BE CONSCIOUS OF THE DAY*

Have a day where you are *AWARE* of how you are creating the day, how you are listening to the day, what it's telling you and how you are responding to what you hear.

- *STAY CONNECTED TO SOURCE*

As often as you can through the day reinforce your connection with source that indeed *YOU ARE GOD!* It's keeping you logged in for the day and doing this aligns you with the guidance that you all have through your lives from source and the energies that work with us. It's also a simple way of evolving your body's relationship with the higher part of us.

- *PRACTICE SOME OR ALL OF THE QUALITIES YOU POSSESS*

What a great way to affirm who you are and to create more!

- *SHOW AN ACT OF KINDNESS TO SOMEONE*

You are here to look out for each other so by expressing some act of kindness or finding some way of serving another human being is a way of loving which is vital for all of us to feel and express.

- *EVEN IF YOU DON'T AGREE WITH SOMEONE'S PERSPECTIVE, SHOW RESPECT*

This doesn't mean you can't have an opinion but respect that others have one as well. It's very easy to become indignant about someone else's perspective if you are not respecting their right to have one. Your response or reaction tells you about yourself, not the person. Know when to walk away or say nothing: it's useful to keep your opinions to yourself at times.

- *THIS IS A LIFE YOU HAVE CHOSEN, IT IS YOUR DEAL*

As odd as it may seem to some people, no one else had a hand in making your life deals. You have always had complete sovereignty over everything. One can struggle with this notion, as most believe the deals you make in life are influenced by others and outside circumstances, but circumstances and people only occur because of you. The New Earth Energy carries a frequency that amplifies the ways you can make the best deals in life. If you are willing to be a participant in this energy then *What Was* does not come into the picture. The New Earth Energy has nothing to do with what has passed. Using the new energy takes you away from the old ways and what you were. It encourages you to live in a fulfilling way, it shows you productive choices and makes it uncomplicated when it comes to making the deals in your life.

- *LOVE, BE LOVED AND BE DIVINE*

Love is the word that is used to define the ultimate vibration of life.

When you are loved, you are given life, when you love back, you are giving life.

When you love yourself, you are standing on the point of creation energy, and you align with your divinity when you give this love to yourselves. This love gives you the feeling of how you are connected to everything and it shows you how you and all are carried by this energy through life and directed in wonderous ways.

Love empowers and heals; it calms us down and lights us up. Love encourages us to advance all your potentials and it is the vibration that makes most sense.

Why does it make most sense?

Love is what God feels.

GOD knows no other feeling but love and so it is the *ULTIMATE FEELING*. When you engage with love it will organize all your other human emotions in such a way where you will only benefit. Creating from the ultimate feeling gives you a more definitive platform on which to create your life. (…) The soul knows where the power comes from and without the energy of love the soul feels detached from life and struggles through the body. (…) and regardless of life being positive or negative by approaching everything with love you gain a greater understanding. Therein lies the challenge then, to find love through adversity as much as through the productive events of life. That's a massive thing to face when humanity is used to being angry at adversity. Many people would find it very difficult to find love in brutality, abuse, negativity. I don't believe for a moment that approaching adverse situations with love is showing an insensitivity or indifference to suffering but it must empower some part of your soul that shows us a way to cope better and direct us toward positive outcomes. You have made conflict a constant in your lives, be it through association or your own self-inflicted conflicts.

Conflict seems to be something that you accept whereas love is something to attain like a reward that you have to earn because of the conflicts you have been through.

Why earn the right to the ultimate feeling when it is freely given?

Inflicting upon us ideas that harbor feelings of guilt and unworthiness seems to be a major conflict for a lot of people. I don't believe the world needs to be like this anymore. Perhaps in the past it was like that because that's where you are as a collective, but I really believe that you have moved away from the idea of that energy as a constant in your lives. That way of thinking and believing has nothing to do with New Earth Energy and that's why you question and react against it, as intrinsically your souls know you have advanced and find no think in such a manner. In the (past) (…) conflict was an unvarying part of life and accepted. That was your history as it was then, people still feeling the need to conquer the Earth and each other. And yet where have all the conflicts through your history actually taken us? Empires come and go, beliefs do the same, and so do your lifetimes. Some things however, remain consistent like the energy of love (…).

CONCLUSION

In conclusion, learn how to empower yourself by utilizing the immense resources available to you. Do not dilute your power to manifest by mixing it with fear or arrogance and ego. True modesty is knowing your real worth. When you do, you will be able to ask the universe for what you need and the universe will move heaven and earth to fulfill your need.

Allama Iqbal, a Pakistani poet, philosopher and politician stated in his poetry:

Khudi ko kar buland itna

Ki har taqdeer se pehle

Khuda bande se khud puchhe

Bata teri raza kya hai?

Translation:

Elevate your 'self' to such heights

That before each destiny

God Himself asks man

Tell me what is your wish?

As difficult as you may find it to believe that life could really be that simple, remember a child who asks politely and accepts his parents' answer, even though it may be 'no' at times, is more likely to get what he wants or asks for than the one who makes demands and throws tantrums…at least from loving and confident parents. Parents who are fearful of losing their child's love if they refuse to comply, will give in. God is a loving parent, not a fearful one, so in His universe, love is the currency that works, even tough love, so there is no place for fear. If you are constantly struggling, some honest self-reflection may provide the answers. While you are learning to trust and replace fear with love, you may be frustrated or find yourself trusting the wrong person. In that case, look again and look for signs you may have missed or messages you may have misread. Know that love and gratitude are the only things that propel the universe to rise to fulfill your wishes.

Know that you are supported.

Walk in faith with your 'team' and enjoy the journey!

Acknowledgements

Many thanks go out to everyone who chose to be a part of this book by sharing their stories. It helped tremendously in validating that we can all receive help from our angels, guides, and teachers even though they are invisible to us.

In all humility, I gratefully acknowledge the help of my own team of invisible helpers in making various choices and receiving guidance along the way.

Thank you to everyone who has been part of my journey and in their own ways and capacities have helped me become who I am and do what I do.

Special thanks to my family who patiently supported me in innumerable ways.

About the Author

Pam Grewall was a teacher. She is a spiritual life coach. She also enjoys being a grandmother. She can be reached via her website www.pamgrewall.com

Printed in the United States
by Baker & Taylor Publisher Services